"*Letting Go of Your Ex* is an expertly crafted self-help guide that will assist anyone struggling to get over a former love. Based on a cognitive behavioral conceptualization of addiction, Cortney Soderlind Warren skillfully helps readers understand their post-breakup symptoms of heartache while teaching practical skills to facilitate healing. Infused with examples that anyone who's fallen [in love will relate to, it offers] readers an empathic path to growth and empowerment."

 —**Phillip Levendusky, PhD, ABPP**, faculty
  Harvard Medical School

"For people suffering in the emotional black hole of love addiction, Cortney Soderlind Warren provides a path forward to a safe place, grounded in one's values. She creatively adapts cognitive behavioral therapy (CBT) skills to guide therapists in a structured yet flexible way to help their clients transform themselves from the inside out. Using a practical approach with empathy, Warren instills hope that healthy mutual love and fulfillment are possible."

 —**Edmund C. Neuhaus, PhD, ABPP**, assistant clinical professor in
  the department of psychiatry at Harvard Medical School

"There are many resources to help clients with their intimate relationships, but few to guide them when those relationships end. This wise and sensitive book by Cortney Soderlind Warren fills the gap—supporting clients through a three-part process of understanding their pain, examining beliefs and early experiences contributing to their distress, and navigating steps toward letting go and moving forward in a healthy way. Readers will grow and prosper!"

 —**Douglas K. Snyder, PhD**, professor in the department of psychological
  and brain sciences at Texas A&M University, coauthor of *Getting Past
  the Affair*, and coeditor of *Clinical Handbook of Couple Therapy*

"Every once in a while, a book comes along that fits several much-needed criteria in the pantheon of self-help texts. Cortney Soderlind Warren combines a compassionate point of view from her work as an esteemed author and clinician, pairing her personal experience with her years of clinical, research, and academic expertise. Filled with case studies and pragmatic exercises, this book is for anyone who has ever felt addicted in romance."

 —**Patrick Ross Scott, PhD, LCSW, DCSW, LFAPA**, adjunct assistant
  professor of psychiatry at the Kirk Kerkorian School of Medicine at the
  University of Nevada, Las Vegas (UNLV); president of the Association of
  Integrative Psychology; and executive vice president and clinical director
  of Heads UP Guidance and Wellness Centers of Nevada

"Cortney Soderlind Warren's evidence-based approach to healing after a breakup is practical and effective. Anyone struggling with difficulty moving forward after a relationship loss will find comfort in this inspiring read, which helps readers to know they are not alone, and gives them empowering solutions for letting go."

 —**Judy Ho, PhD, ABPP, ABPdN, CFMHE**, clinical and forensic
  neuropsychologist, tenured professor at Pepperdine University, and
  author of *Stop Self-Sabotage*

"For those struggling with post-breakup emotions and behaviors, Cortney Soderlind Warren's book is like having a therapist in your hand. She walks the reader through the process of CBT in a seamless fashion, interwoven with example vignettes which truly bring the book to life. Her embedded worksheets will be a gift to readers embroiled in 'EXAHOLIC' patterns. Warren truly has a gift of breaking down complex concepts into easily digestible bites, as she invites the reader on a journey of self-discovery."

—**Lisa Durette, MD, DFAPA, DFAACAP**, vice chair of the Kirk
Kerkorian School of Medicine at the UNLV department of psychiatry
and behavioral health

"*Letting Go of Your Ex* is an engaging book for anyone who finds themselves addicted to love and struggling to let go. Cortney Soderlind Warren breaks down the healing journey into three easy-to-follow stages with exercises to help you along the way. This book is an excellent first step toward building a confident and authentic self."

—**Linda Castillo, PhD**, psychologist, and professor of counseling psychology
at Texas A&M University

"Cortney Soderlind Warren eloquently captures the inner psyche of a person who is in the throes of a painful breakup. Using case studies, science, and practical tools, Warren helps the addicted person gain insight into why they feel the way they do, and how they can free themselves from emotional heartbreak. This is definitely a book I will recommend to my patients struggling to get over an ex."

—**Robi Ludwig, PsyD**, psychotherapist, author, TV expert, and creator and
host of *Talking Live with Dr. Robi Ludwig* and the *Byte Size* podcast

"For anyone who has fallen head over heels in love only to find it's taking an eternity to stop thinking about your ex, this book is for you. Compassionately narrated life stories meet empirically supported techniques for letting go of your ex."

—**Andrea Goeglein, PhD**, cofounder of Serving Success; cohost of the
Hey Boss Lady! podcast; and coauthor of the *Don't Die* inspirational book series

"Cortney Soderlind Warren's book explains how CBT skills can be used to address a love addition to an ex-spouse, partner, or love interest in a way that makes the techniques accessible to anyone. The case studies provide fascinating insights into the real-life applications of CBT. Warren also explains the underlying neurological basis of love addiction, and provides a compelling case for using CBT to address this problem."

—**Nancy Raymond, MD**, board-certified psychiatrist who has served on the
faculty at two Midwestern medical schools over her thirty-year career

Letting Go of Your Ex

**CBT Skills to
Heal the Pain
of a Breakup
& Overcome
Love Addiction**

Cortney Soderlind Warren, PhD

New Harbinger Publications, Inc.

Publisher's Note

NEW HARBINGER PUBLICATIONS is a registered trademark of New Harbinger Publications, Inc.

New Harbinger Publications is an employee-owned company.

Cover design by Amy Daniel; Acquired by Ryan Buresh;
Edited by James Lainsbury

FSC
www.fsc.org
MIX
Paper from
responsible sources
FSC® C011935

Library of Congress Cataloging-in-Publication Data

Names: Warren, Cortney S., author.
Title: Letting go of your ex : CBT skills to heal the pain of a breakup and overcome love addiction / Cortney S. Warren, PhD, ABPP.
Description: Oakland, CA : New Harbinger Publications, [2023] | Includes bibliographical references.
Identifiers: LCCN 2022044895 | ISBN 9781648480379 (trade paperback)
Subjects: LCSH: Relationship addiction--Popular works. | Relationship addiction--Treatment--Popular works. | Cognitive therapy--Popular works. | BISAC: FAMILY & RELATIONSHIPS / Divorce & Separation | PSYCHOLOGY / Mental Health
Classification: LCC RC552.R44 W37 2023 | DDC 616.89/1425--dc23/eng/20221013
LC record available at https://lccn.loc.gov/2022044895

Printed in the United States of America

25   24   23

10   9   8   7   6   5   4   3   2   1   First Printing

Contents

Acknowledgments

I couldn't have written this book without the incredible support of many people in my personal and professional life. To my mother, Dr. Karen J. Warren, who taught me to think critically. To my husband, Cal, and our children, Isabella and Kane, who cheered me on as I took time away to write. To my many esteemed mentors at Macalester College, Texas A&M University, McLean Hospital, Harvard Medical School, and the American Psychological Association's Minority Fellowship Program who've helped me explore the human experience. To my students and colleagues whose work continues to expand our understanding of mental health. To the editors at New Harbinger for their excellent feedback on this book throughout my writing process. And, perhaps most importantly, to the clients who've let me into their internal worlds over the last twenty years. I'm immensely grateful.

Note About Case Examples

This book includes many stories and case examples. Although all reflect common experiences of people who feel addicted to their ex, I've edited, modified, or changed some of the content to ensure that no individual person can be identified. Any resemblance to specific people or events is purely coincidental.

Foreword

I've known Dr. Cortney Warren for over twenty years, although for the first five years of our initial mentor-mentee relationship she was just Cortney—a bright, enthusiastic, idealistic student who craved knowledge and was hungry to improve the world. I'm happy to report that sixteen years after receiving a PhD, Dr. Warren has not only retained all the enthusiasm and youthful energy that Cortney brought to Texas A&M, but also gained prodigious wisdom through hard work and inspiring vision. Dr. Warren has certainly made important inroads into bettering the lives of others, including her own students and mentees, clients, and social media followers.

Letting Go of Your Ex: CBT Skills to Heal the Pain of a Breakup and Overcome Love Addiction is an accessible, easy-to-read guide that helps therapists and clients follow an evidence-based path leading to emotional and relational freedom. Dr. Warren uses personal, intimate stories mined from her own and her clients' personal experiences to illustrate and, more importantly, normalize and humanize the universality of adaptive and maladaptive romantic love. Whereas mature love integrates and balances needing, giving, companionship, and romance, immature love is characterized by possession, power, disappointment, and perversion. Immature love fanatically upholds the notion that love is blind and beyond control. Dr. Warren translates into familiar language expert knowledge to show that romantic love may become a shackle that limits almost every aspect of a person's life, repeatedly triggers "uncontrollable" behaviors, and brings about pain and suffering. Through her impeccable prose, we learn that immature, maladaptive love becomes uniquely debilitating and saddening when the subject of our "love" does not reciprocate or is unreachable.

One need not take a huge leap to appreciate her approach. For me, an investigator of drug and food addiction for many decades, the similarities between being "madly" in love and being addicted to a drug are easy to catch. For instance, as the smoker addicted to nicotine lights up their first cigarette shortly after waking and continues to smoke throughout the day, a person addicted to love may wake up thinking about the person they are in love with and likely continue to think about them throughout the day. The smoker may or may not be aware of their smoking addiction, but they will certainly notice their cigarette cravings and subsequent frustration when their cigarettes run out, or when smoking is not allowed. Similarly, the person stuck in an unreciprocated—unrealizable—relationship will crave the company of their loved one, particularly when their target is unreachable, and even malign their partner, feeling saddened and frustrated because they can't have what they want.

Eventually, and hopefully, individuals addicted to cigarettes may learn that smoking is harmful to their health and become aware of their need to quit, giving up smoking for good. Similarly, the person involved in a maladaptive romantic relationship would be well advised to realize they are stuck and must free themselves from the tyranny of their own affections—more easily said than done! It is well known that the average ex-smoker self-initiates nearly a dozen serious quit attempts before succeeding at continuous, long-term abstinence. Unsurprisingly, the long-term success of smokers who attempt abstinence without formal/professional help is abysmally low. Conversely, smokers who seek formal help, particularly help that incorporates CBT (cognitive behavioral therapy) skills, exponentially increase their chances of smoking-cessation success.

One may imagine that without formal help the person addicted to love will have great difficulty understanding the dynamics of their frustrated and damaging obsessions. I undoubtedly recall my first-ever practicum client when I was a first-year clinical psychology student. My client was a bright engineering senior who had been recently rejected by his first love. He was left kneeling with a huge diamond between his thumb and index finger in the dining room of the town's only French restaurant. Unfortunately for me, and particularly for my client, *Letting Go of Your Ex* has arrived about thirty-five years too late. Fortunately for clients and therapists today, this book will help them understand and recognize—through the use of real stories and CBT scientific principles—how and why people are stuck and suffer from love addiction. Moreover, Dr. Warren maps out a proven route to reclaim the afflicted person's autonomy and freedom—their best chance at finding true, mature, adaptive romantic love.

—Dr. Antonio Cepeda-Benito, PhD
Department of Psychological Science
University of Vermont

The Path to Letting Go of Your Ex

New beginnings are often disguised as painful endings.

—Lao Tzu

Like you, I've struggled to get over an ex. I mean, *seriously struggled.* At no time were my internal battles more obvious than the first time I fell in love. From the moment I saw him walking across the grassy field that led to our dorm my first week in college, I was intrigued. He was handsome and athletic, but that wasn't what grabbed my attention. There was an unexplainable spark, a chemistry that shivered through me when he glanced my way and flashed his dimpled smile. Living on the same floor, we saw each other almost every day. I smiled coyly in blushed delight when he passed me in the hall. After we started talking and studying together after class, I wanted to be around him more and more. I'd never felt so captivated by another person. I felt alive when he was near. Soon, we were a couple and I was madly in love.

The problem was that I wasn't well equipped to be in love *at all.* I brought a mountain of baggage with me that burdened our relationship in ways I couldn't see and didn't understand. After about two years together, he told me he wanted to be less serious. Essentially, we were breaking up and I was devastated. At first, I couldn't believe it. We shared so many intimate experiences, passionate nights, inside jokes, and plans for our future. How could this be happening? Panic coursed through me as I racked my brain for answers, desperate to fix whatever was broken so we could get back together. All I wanted was to be with him, talk to him, touch him, understand what went wrong—anything to feel close again and make the pain go away. As the reality of our breakup set in, I was overcome with emotion. What had started as panicky excitement when I ran into him on campus quickly morphed into intense anger when I thought about the now-broken promises he'd made while we were together. Sitting alone in my room at night, I'd anxiously wait for a call, study old letters, and relive conversations we'd had in my own mind. In the end, I found myself on a seemingly never-ending rollercoaster ride of a fragmented romance that occupied my heart for years. Until one day, long after our first breakup, when I realized that I needed to let go of the ghost of my ex if I were ever going to fully enjoy my life again.

If you're reading this book, you're probably all too familiar with the heartbreaking misery that can come from losing a romantic partner. And you're not alone. At some point in our lives, almost all of us will suffer an excruciatingly painful breakup that absolutely rocks our world. It may be so all-consuming that you feel *addicted to your ex* (Bobby 2015; Costa et al. 2019; Peele and Brodsky 1975). Desperate to reconnect and understand what happened, you can become fixated on your former lover as if you need them to survive. As if your life has lost all meaning without them by your side. As if you no longer have purpose or value on your own. Like me, you may have had a rock-bottom "aha" moment when you realized that you can't continue living like this. If that's true for you, your healing journey can start right now. And it begins with understanding love addiction.

What's Love Addiction?

When you think about love, you probably don't think of it as addictive. Alcoholic, workaholic, shopaholic, chocoholic—you've probably heard these terms to describe people struggling with addictive tendencies toward alcohol, work, shopping, or even certain foods like chocolate. But the idea of being addicted to a former lover—being an *exaholic*—may be new to you. Yet emerging research suggests that you can feel addicted to a person because of your basic human need for love (Fisher 2016).

Pioneering neurobiological research indicates that the very natural process of falling in love *is* an addictive one (Earp et al. 2017; Fisher et al. 2016; Sussman 2010). Romantic love stimulates a very old part of our brain that's associated with survival; it's referred to as the *dopaminergic reward pathway* or *pleasure center* (Filbey 2019; Fisher et al. 2002). When you act in ways that help our species survive, your brain and body reward you by making the activity feel good. You're actually evolutionarily and biologically driven to find a mate, have sex, make babies, and stay around your partner long enough to ensure the survival of your child (Fisher 2016; Tobore 2020). And, when you fall in love with someone who wants you, feeling addicted to a lover doesn't seem problematic. Quite the contrary: it's euphoric! Problems emerge when you fall for someone who isn't healthy for you or doesn't want you back. Then the addictive nature of love can throw you into a miserable cycle of symptoms that harms your emotional, physical, psychological, and spiritual well-being.

Although love addiction isn't a clinical diagnosis or mental illness, the experience of feeling addicted to a person or behavior—like gambling, gaming, pornography, or sex—has been explored for decades (Grant et al. 2010; Kim et al. 2020; Peele and Brodsky 1975; Sussman, Lisha, and Griffiths 2011). In general terms, love addiction is a maladaptive pattern of thoughts, feelings, and behaviors driven by an excessive focus on a current or former romantic partner that seriously impairs one's well-being (Sanches and John 2019; Sussman 2010). And, if you've ever felt addicted to an ex, you probably know the insidious symptoms all too well. Your ex becomes the single-most dominant focus of your life, consuming your energy at the expense of almost everything else. You yearn to see them, talk to them, touch them, and understand what went wrong. Desperate to feel close again, you think about them all the time and act in ways that ultimately make you feel worse, like constantly checking your phone to see if they called or driving by their home hoping to catch a glimpse of what they're doing. Over time these relentless symptoms make you doubt yourself—your integrity, your identity, even your fundamental value. Feeling addicted to an ex makes letting them go excruciatingly hard even when you rationally want to move on.

How This Book Can Help You

The good news is, there's hope; you don't have to live like this anymore. There are many highly effective skills you can use to heal the pain of this breakup. Based on a treatment known as cognitive behavioral therapy, or CBT, this book will teach you how your thoughts, feelings, and behaviors interact to affect your experience of this breakup (J. S. Beck 2021; Tolin 2016). Simply put, how you think about your breakup affects the way you feel and want to act. When you understand the unhelpful thought-feeling-behavior patterns that keep you stuck, you can practice skills to stop them. Not only will this make you feel better, but the energy you've spent suffering can be reinvested into creating a fulfilling future. Grounded in decades of data-based research, CBT is one of the most effective psychological treatments for addictions and mental health struggles of many kinds (A. T. Beck et al. 1979; J. S. Beck 2021; Hofmann et al. 2012; Tolin 2016). Practicing CBT skills can even rewire your brain and change your neurobiological reactions over time (Filbey 2019; Marwood et al. 2018).

By the time you finish this book you'll have learned:

- How and why love can function like an addiction

- The primary symptoms of an exaholic breakup, how they operate in your life, and specific skills to stop them

- Common flawed ways of thinking about your ex that keep you stuck, and how to challenge them

- Core beliefs about love that you developed in childhood and harm your romantic relationships as an adult—including the one with your ex

- How to create the next phase of your life by grieving your breakup and making value-based choices moving forward

This book is organized into three parts that focus on helping you understand your symptoms, exploring how you got here, and creating a brighter future. As is important for anyone struggling to overcome psychological pain, our first goal is to stop your most distressing symptoms. Think of part 1 of this book as the triage phase of your recovery; as if you're being rushed into an emergency room with a deep cut, our initial goal is to examine your wound, assess the damage, and stop the bleeding. So, part 1 details the telltale signs of a love-addicted breakup, helps you assess your symptoms, and teaches you specific CBT skills that stop your harmful thought-feeling-behavior patterns.

As you learn to effectively combat your symptoms, our next goal is to uncover how you got here in the first place: after we stop your bleeding we need to understand when, why, and how you got wounded. So, in part 2 we'll explore how your thinking about this breakup fuels your addictive symptoms. You'll learn to challenge untrue and unhelpful thoughts about yourself, your ex, and love that damage your romantic relationships. As you do, you'll embrace a more accurate, self-enhancing perspective on your romantic life, this breakup, and you.

Finally, we'll explore what you want for yourself moving forward. After your cut heals, you'll still have a scar. You won't forget your ex and you can't erase the past, but you can learn to see your wound differently. In part 3 we'll look at your breakup as a grieving process that you can overcome through forgiveness, by taking responsibility for your role, and by making amends. You'll identify your core values and use them to guide your choices moving forward—including how they can help you when you're ready to start dating again. We'll end by measuring how much you've changed and by preparing you to fight off any stubborn symptoms that may reemerge as you step into the next great chapter of your life.

This process—from immediate symptom relief to deeper self-exploration to creating a more meaningful future—requires that you continually engage in three basic steps: *awareness*, *assessment*, and *action*. To heal from this breakup, you must develop honest *awareness* of yourself and your symptoms. This means learning to notice your reactions and pausing to acknowledge them as honestly as possible in the moment. Second, you must *assess* how current and past learning are contributing to your suffering—that is, understanding how you're unintentionally making your struggles worse through your responses, thinking patterns, beliefs, and behaviors. Finally, you must take *action* to change. Although understanding your symptoms is critical to overcoming love addiction, you also have to do things differently to break the patterns that keep you stuck. Together, becoming aware of your experience, assessing how you got here, and taking action to change is the process that'll ultimately heal your pain and inspire you to authentically move forward.

Creating a Brighter Future

Loving another person is an incredibly vulnerable and complicated experience. We can fall so madly in love that breaking up throws us into a damaging addictive cycle of symptoms that's incredibly difficult to stop. As you read this book, I encourage you not to be judgmental or harsh toward yourself, your ex, or your past. The healing process isn't intended to breed resentment, bitterness, or fixation on past pain. Instead, this is a journey of observation and personal growth. Think of it as an introspective voyage into yourself to explore how you relate to your ex and why in a more comprehensive way. As painful as this breakup may be to live through, you can turn it into one of the most positive transformational experiences of your life (Kansky and Allen 2018).

I know that you may feel absolutely miserable right now. You may be struggling to get through each day, maybe even through each minute of the day. It may seem like nothing good could possibly come from this experience, but I'm here to tell you that something can. There's always a gift in life's most painful moments because *distress is one of the biggest predictors of therapeutic change.* You're more likely to evolve and grow when you feel so bad that you can't afford to stay the same (Kirouac and Witkiewitz 2017; Uckelstam et al. 2019). Don't get me wrong, letting go of your ex won't be easy. This kind of work takes daily practice and deliberate effort. But as your ex stops being the center of your world, you can emerge as a stronger, more authentic version of yourself. One who knows what you really want. Who recognizes your value as a person. Who's resilient and dedicated to living a fulfilling life with or without a romantic partner. Although it may sound strange, getting over your ex has very little to do with them; it's all about understanding and transforming yourself. And I'm here to help you do it. Let's begin.

Part 1

When Losing a Lover Devastates You

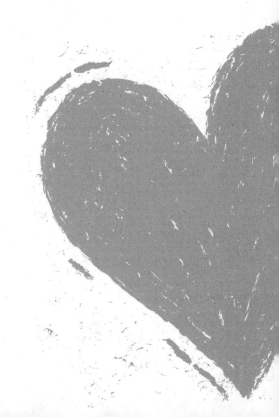

CHAPTER 1

Feeling Addicted to Your Ex

It's been two weeks since my boyfriend broke up with me. I was completely shocked—I didn't see it coming. We'd been together nine months and I thought we were really connecting. Now, I'm a mess. I can't stop thinking about him. All I want is to talk to him, understand what happened, and go back to the way it was. I can't eat or sleep. I cry all the time. I feel like I'm losing my mind.

I was eighteen years old when I met the love of my life. Now, twenty years later, I still haven't gotten over her. I'm married to another woman and have two kids, but I still think about her every day. I feel guilty because my feelings for my wife aren't like my feelings for my ex. Sometimes I even secretly scroll through my ex's pictures online just to see what she's doing. I don't know how to move on.

I've been living in my own internal hell since my boyfriend and I broke up. Even though it's been over three months since we talked, I still look at my phone constantly hoping to see his name pop up. It's like I'm obsessed with him. I feel so pathetic. I can't live like this anymore. I need help. I need to let go of my ex.

Do these descriptions sound familiar to you? Could some of these exact same words come out of your mouth when describing your ex? If so, let me start by assuring you that you're not alone. I've been there. Millions of others around the world have been there. Breakups affect people of all ages, races, ethnic groups, genders, cultures, sexual orientations, and religions. Because as humans *we're driven to love* (Fisher 2016; Fisher et al. 2016). If you're lucky enough to have experienced the bliss of falling in love, you know that sometimes it comes with a cost: breaking up can send you into an addictive downward spiral of heartache, loss, and despair.

The truth is that the very natural process of falling in love can look and feel like you're addicted to your mate (Earp et al. 2017; Reynaud et al. 2010; Sussman 2010). You meet that special someone and become enchanted. A rush of physical, sexual, and emotional attraction flows through you when they're near. You want to be around them all the time because you feel incredible when you're together. It's like you can't get enough of them! Even when you're not together, you're thinking about them, talking about them, and fantasizing about the next time you can see them. Your world starts to revolve around your lover as if they were the sun.

And then, you break up. Maybe the spark that was once electrifying fizzled or disappeared completely. Maybe you had dramatic fights that created irreconcilable rifts. Maybe one of you wanted kids and the other didn't. Maybe your ex cheated and you couldn't forgive them. Maybe your cultural backgrounds were too different to make it work. Maybe your ex didn't love you the way you love them. Maybe you just grew apart. Or maybe you have no idea what happened; one day your lover just ghosted you and left without explanation. Whatever the reason, when loved ones ask you how you're doing, words like *lost, miserable, gutted,* and *heartbroken* come to mind. Because this person who once occupied your heart is gone and you don't know how to move on without them.

As miserable as you might feel right now, your symptoms don't mean something's wrong with you; they mean you lost someone you loved deeply. In this chapter, we'll explore the primary symptoms of a love-addicted breakup, what causes them, and how they may be negatively affecting your life. The first step to letting go of your ex and healing the pain of this breakup is becoming acutely aware of your experience. As clichéd as it sounds, knowledge is power: the more you understand what you're going through, the more power you have to change it. So, we'll start your healing journey by exploring the primary symptoms of an exaholic breakup.

Symptoms of an Exaholic Breakup

Going through a love-addicted breakup can leave you heartbroken and disoriented. As the pleasure you felt being around your ex is ripped away and your life crumbles before your eyes, you enter a state of withdrawal that feels horrible (Bobby 2015; Fisher et al. 2016). Searching for ways to feel better, you become laser-focused on the perceived cause of your anguish: your ex. An intense desire to feel close to them again consumes you and drives the characteristic symptoms of an exaholic breakup: obsessive thinking, cravings for contact, emotional distress, and harmful acting-out behaviors. Let's explore each of these in more detail.

During an exaholic breakup you're likely to experience *intrusive and obsessive thinking about your ex* (Field 2017; Perilloux and Buss 2008). You may find yourself ruminating about them, analyzing them, and fantasizing about them almost all the time. Anything from reminiscing about sweet moments you shared to reliving heated arguments to rehearsing what you'd really like to say to them now. Your mind may run wild imagining their life today—where they are, who they're dating, and whether they still think about you. These thoughts may be incessant, consuming your mental space and bombarding your mind from the moment you wake up in the morning until you fall asleep at night. You may desperately want to turn off your brain and stop thinking about them, but as much as you try, you can't.

These unwanted thoughts are often accompanied by overwhelming *cravings for contact with your ex* (Costa et al. 2019; Reynaud et al. 2010). It feels like you're being magnetically pulled back to them. You urgently want to see them, be around them, talk to them, yell at them, hug them, punish them, or get information about what they're doing now. Your whole body yearns to be close again because it feels like your misery would all go away if you could just get back together, get justice, or more fully understand what went wrong so you can fix it.

As if the obsessive thinking and cravings weren't tormenting enough, you're also probably feeling extremely *emotionally distressed and reactive* (Barutcu and Aydin 2013; Field et al. 2011). As you wrestle with the stark reality of your breakup, you may be overcome by a range of deeply upsetting emotions—from profound hurt to sadness, anxiety, anger, frustration, confusion, guilt, and even fear. These intense feelings are often volatile, changing quickly in response to situations you encounter throughout the day (Starcke et al. 2018). When you learn something new about your ex, for example, you may feel curiosity followed by a rush of rage and then profound sorrow. This reactivity leaves you feeling moody and out of control, like a prisoner to your own emotions.

Finally, as your thoughts, cravings, and emotional experiences worsen, you're also more likely to engage in *harmful compulsive and impulsive behaviors* aimed either at feeling closer to your ex or at distracting yourself from your pain (Bakhshani 2014; Field 2017; Luigjes et al. 2019). To feel closer, you might drive past your ex's home, show up at their favorite hangouts, look for details about their new life on social media, or text them repeatedly. When you're at your worst, you may even feel like a stalker sneakily tracking your ex's whereabouts (Fox and Tokunaga 2015; Roberts 2002). Any tidbit of information makes you feel better—even if it ultimately crushes your heart—like seeing a picture of your ex with their new lover. When you can't feel closer, you might try to distract yourself by joining an online dating site or having sex as an emotional diversion. You may even engage in self-destructive behaviors that ultimately hurt you profoundly, like chain-smoking, drinking, or using drugs to excess, gambling too much, binge eating, or cutting yourself (Zarate et al. 2022).

Taken together, these highly unpleasant symptoms leave you feeling like you've lost control of yourself and your life (Bobby 2015; Field 2017). You may have stopped taking care of your basic needs, like eating well, seeing your friends, and being productive at work. Your self-esteem suffers as you question who you are and your desirability as a romantic partner—especially if your ex rejected, left, or cheated on you. You may not recognize yourself anymore because you're feeling so weak and lost. Ultimately, these symptoms make it nearly impossible for you to enjoy your life.

Have you struggled with some of these symptoms? Do you find yourself obsessively thinking about your ex? Experience strong urges to contact them or learn what they're doing now? Feel emotionally distraught and reactive? Act in impulsive or compulsive ways that ultimately hurt you? Feel lost and disempowered? As you think about your experience, it's helpful to see what an exaholic breakup looks like in another person. So, let's consider Maria's story.

When Maria stepped into my office wearing worn-out sweatpants and sporting a disheveled ponytail, it was visibly clear that she was really distressed. She had a forlorn look in her eyes as she told me about her recent breakup with the love of her life, John. As she described her relationship, from their first meeting to that moment in my office, the characteristic and painful symptoms of love addiction emerged. She told her story like this:

I met John on an online dating site. He started messaging me with quirky, funny little comments that made me laugh. After a few weeks, we met in person at a park with our dogs. He was wearing a plaid shirt and shorts; he looked so cute. And he was nice and easy to be around. He seemed to know exactly what to say to make me feel special. The more we hung out, the more I liked him. Even our dogs liked each other! I loved how I felt when I was with him. After years of struggling to meet someone, I thought John was the man of my dreams. I was so happy!

Then everything fell apart. I'm from a big Latino family, and I've always wanted kids. About six months into our relationship, I mustered up the courage to tell John that I wanted to get more serious—to move in together and start building a future. Looking deeply into my eyes, John said that he loved me but wasn't interested in settling down and thought that I understood he didn't want a committed relationship. I was stunned. That night we broke up, and I've been a mess ever since. I think about him all the time. I'm so mad at him, but at the same time I miss him so much. I spend hours sitting in bed reading old messages and checking his social media accounts to see what he's doing. Sometimes I even look at his dating profile to see how many hours it's been since he was last active. I picture him living a glamorous life, going out with new women while I'm here pathetically suffering alone.

Occasionally John texts me or stops by unexpectedly. In those moments I'm so relieved to hear from him that I usually indulge. But after we hook up and he gets ready to leave, I start to panic, pleading with him to take me back or screaming at him for being such a jerk. Then I feel even worse. I'm just a wreck. I have no appetite. I can't sleep. I've isolated myself from my family and friends because I don't want to talk. I'm so embarrassed. I feel lost and broken. He doesn't want me, so why can't I just let him go?

Do you see the characteristic symptoms of a love-addicted breakup in Maria's story? After falling for John hard and then breaking up, Maria has become fixated on him. She can't stop thinking about him, craves his attention, feels extremely emotionally distressed, and acts in ways that ultimately make her feel worse, like continuing to have sex with him despite being broken up and scanning his online dating profile for recent activity. Maria's symptoms dramatically affect her well-being: she's struggling to sleep, isolating herself from loved ones, and questioning her self-worth. In the end, Maria's stuck in love-addicted heartache without a clear picture of how to move on.

Do you relate to Maria's experience? Let's pause for a moment to explore your story of love and loss.

EXERCISE: Telling Your Story

To start your healing process, I want you to tell your relationship story from the day you met your ex until now. Writing can be healing in and of itself because it helps you process your experience and see the big picture of your relationship journey in a safe, confidential way (Lepore and Greenberg 2002; Primeau, Servaty-Seib, and Enersen 2013). In fact, I want you to get a journal dedicated to doing the exercises in this book. Save all your work, including this writing, because you'll use it to reflect back on and track your improvement over time. This can be your first entry!

Using Maria's story as an example, start by describing how you met your ex. What stands out about your first interaction? Where were you? How did you feel and what did you do? Then describe the course of your relationship until now. Take your time to reflect on the most memorable moments. Write as though you're talking to a trusted friend or therapist. Hold nothing back because no one will ever read your story unless you choose to share it. Although it may be difficult to acknowledge the blissful and devastating aspects of your romance, it's often an enormous relief to get the heart-wrenching details out of your head and onto paper.

After writing your story, look at your descriptions. Do you see any symptoms of love addiction? Maybe it's obvious to you that you're experiencing an exaholic breakup. Or maybe you're still a little unsure about whether you feel addicted to your ex or not. Remember that love addiction isn't a clinical diagnosis, so you don't need to give yourself a label. That said, part of the healing process is becoming aware of your symptoms so you can assess them and take action to change. The biggest indicator that you're struggling with an exaholic breakup is that *you're fixated on your ex to the degree that it's harming your well-being*. So, to really unpack your experience, we'll need to explore the toll this breakup has had on your quality of life.

How Being Addicted to Your Ex Hurts You

As we saw in Maria's story, and as you may be experiencing now, going through an exaholic breakup can leave you with devastating and relentless symptoms that dominate your life. At a minimum, your ex and this breakup become the central focus of your life, consuming your energy at the expense of almost everything else (Sanches and John 2019; Sussman, Lisha, and

Griffiths 2011; Zarate et al. 2022). Considering that you're broken up—maybe not by your choosing—this fixation alone is brutal.

Furthermore, the destructive symptoms of an exaholic breakup—the intrusive thinking, cravings, emotional distress, and harmful behaviors—have probably wreaked havoc on your general well-being and ability to function productively (Field 2017; Reimer and Estrada 2021). You may be unmotivated to do things that used to be fun and meaningful to you, like seeing friends, making appearances at family events, or pursuing your favorite hobbies. You may be floundering at work or school because it's just too hard to focus or even show up. Your physical health may be suffering because you're eating poorly, drinking a lot, chain-smoking, acting in sexually promiscuous ways, not cleaning your home, or exercising too much or not at all.

You're probably also feeling emotionally unstable and unsettled (Perilloux and Buss 2008). You may be deeply depressed, angry, resentful, or anxious most of the time. And, as we discussed earlier, you're likely to be more emotionally reactive than usual; you may feel like a ticking time bomb that might explode at any moment (Starcke et al. 2018). Your body may also be reacting to the stress of this breakup: you may sleep poorly, have vivid and upsetting dreams, feel nauseated or sick to your stomach, struggle to concentrate, and experience panic or crying spells (Field 2017; Field et al. 2011; Fisher 2016).

Perhaps even worse, this breakup may leave you feeling exposed and vulnerable, as though you've lost your secure base and no longer have control over the direction of your life (Perilloux and Buss 2008). You may be struggling to find your identify and purpose now that your ex is gone. Your self-esteem has probably taken a hit as you process lingering embarrassment, guilt, and regret over the way your relationship ended. We're generally not our best selves when we're in tremendous pain. So, if you lied, became aggressive, or compromised your own moral values—as many of us do in the throes of a love-addicted breakup—you may feel tremendous shame about your behavior. Not to mention that if your ex rejected, humiliated, or mistreated you in some way, you're now dealing with the deeply cutting repercussions these experiences wrought on your self-image.

Have you noticed any of these symptoms in yourself? Have you lost motivation and interest in things that used to matter? Are you underperforming at work or school? Have you stopped taking care of your physical and emotional health? Do you feel like you've lost yourself? As you consider the ways this breakup has hurt your well-being and functioning in life, it'll help to get a more detailed assessment of your symptoms so we can work to address them.

EXERCISE: Are You an Exaholic?

The following Exaholic Assessment Questionnaire will help you identify your symptoms and assess to what degree they're negatively affecting your life. You can record your responses in your journal or download a copy of this assessment for free at this book's website: http://www.newharbinger.com/50379. Carefully read each statement and respond based on your experience *in the last week*. Rate the accuracy of each item as honestly as you can using the following scale:

1 = not at all true of me	*4 = mostly true of me*
2 = slightly true of me	*5 = completely true of me*
3 = often true of me	

Intrusive and Obsessive Thinking

_____ I think about my ex almost all the time.

_____ Unwanted thoughts of my ex pop into my mind unexpectedly and stay stuck there.

_____ In my mind I relive past experiences I had with my ex or rehearse what I'd like to say to them now.

_____ I want to stop thinking about my ex but can't.

Cravings for Contact

_____ I desperately want to contact my ex (for example, to talk to or see them).

_____ I feel strong urges to connect with my ex even though I know it's going to be a negative interaction (like a fight).

_____ It's almost impossible for me not to contact or seek out information about my ex.

_____ When I'm not in contact with my ex I feel terrible.

Emotional Distress and Reactivity

_____ I'm extremely emotionally distressed because of my breakup.

_____ I struggle to feel happiness or pleasure since my ex and I broke up.

_____ I'm more moody and emotionally reactive since my breakup.

_____ I'm emotionally unable to let go of my ex.

Harmful Compulsive and Impulsive Behaviors

_____ I actively try to contact my ex or do things to feel close to them again (for example, calling them, texting them, or looking through old photos).

_____ I actively try to get information about my ex behind their back (for example, through social media or mutual friends).

_____ I act in ways that ultimately hurt me to feel closer to my ex (for example, driving by their home or having sex with them).

_____ I engage in unhealthy behaviors to distract myself from the pain of this breakup (for example, drinking too much, smoking, or binge eating).

Costs to My Well-Being

_____ I struggle to function in my daily life because I can't get over my ex (for example, I'm not performing as well at work or taking care of my physical health).

_____ I've lost motivation to do things that I used to enjoy because of this breakup (for example, seeing friends or doing my favorite hobbies).

_____ My self-esteem has suffered because of this breakup.

_____ My inability to let go of my ex has made my life unmanageable.

Now, add up the numbers of all twenty items. Your score will range between 20 and 100, with a higher score indicating stronger exaholic symptoms. Since you're reading this book, my guess is that your score is quite high—and that's to be expected. I wrote this book to help you change that! But if your score is low, you probably aren't struggling with love addiction.

Next, identify any items and specific symptoms or general areas (like "cravings for contact" or "emotional distress and reactivity") you rated highly because you'll want to target changing these areas most aggressively. Don't be discouraged if you endorsed most of the items—many people going through breakups experience symptoms at extremely high levels, especially early in their recovery. Save your answers to this assessment because you'll complete it again at the end of the book to see how much you've changed. I also want to emphasize that by telling your story and doing this assessment, you're becoming more *aware* of your symptoms and you've *assessed* their severity and how they're affecting your life. Soon you'll be *acting* to change them. So, you've already started the healing process!

At this point, you may be asking yourself, *Why me?! Why do I feel addicted to my ex?* You may have friends who've never struggled like this through a breakup. Or maybe you've gone through breakups that didn't make you feel this way. Although the answer to this question is incredibly complicated, it's at least due, in part, to what's going on in your brain. So, let's delve into that topic now.

Why Am I Addicted to My Ex?

Vulnerability to addictions of all kinds is a complex interaction of genetic, biological, psychological, and sociocultural factors that we're just beginning to understand and unravel (Filbey 2019; Kwako and Koob 2017; National Institute on Drug Abuse 2019; National Institute on Drug Abuse 2020; Zarate et al. 2022). For example, some people can drink alcohol or gamble and not have it turn into a problematic addictive experience, whereas others can't. Similarly, breakups won't lead to addictive symptoms in some people, whereas for others they will. Even for those of us who are particularly prone to experiencing love addiction, only certain exes will cause symptoms to emerge. In part 2 of this book we'll spend a lot of time exploring some of the important psychological and sociocultural factors that can put people at risk—including how adverse childhood experiences lead to untrue core beliefs and faulty thinking about yourself and others. For now, I want to highlight the biological aspects of addiction that are contributing to your symptoms.

Addictive behavior is associated with stimulation in a very old, survival-based part of the brain commonly referred to as the *pleasure center*, or *dopaminergic reward pathway* (Blum et al. 2012; Filbey 2019; Koob and Volkow 2010). Our bodies release feel-good chemicals and hormones when we engage in biologically desirable behaviors, like having sex and eating. This is because, from an evolutionary perspective, these behaviors increased the likelihood that we'd survive as a species. So, your body encourages you to engage in these behaviors again and again by making you feel wonderful when you do (Koob and Volkow 2010)!

Emerging neurobiological research has shown that falling in love can stimulate this same area of the brain. When you experience romantic love, a host of neurotransmitters and hormones are released or inhibited (including dopamine, serotonin, oxytocin, and some stress hormones), making you feel euphoric and focused on your lover (Fisher, Aron, and Brown 2005; Fisher 2016; Reynaud et al. 2010). In essence, your lover becomes a drug: they bring pleasure and decrease pain. If you then break up, however, the loss of your lover throws you into a state of withdrawal that feels miserable. Desperate to feel better, your body, heart, and mind fixate on being close to your now ex because being with them felt wonderful and being away from them feels terrible. As you unsuccessfully attempt to reconnect, you begin to experience obsessive thinking, cravings, emotional distress, and a desire to act in harmful ways. So, biologically, it makes sense why it's so hard to let go of your ex. Not to mention that your entire lifestyle's changing, which can be jarring and emotionally heartbreaking all at once!

The dramatic psychological shifts you're experiencing right now lead me to one very important question: *How ready are you to let go of your ex and move on without them?* Your answer is critical, because how committed you are to changing will largely determine how quickly you recover from this breakup (Norcross, Krebs, and Prochaska 2011). So, let's prepare for that commitment now.

Committing to Change

To really heal from this breakup, you need to *commit to letting go of your ex by practicing the skills in this book.* Why's this so important? As we'll explore in depth in the next chapter, moving on requires that you respond to your symptoms in a new way. Over the course of this book, you're going to learn an arsenal of skills designed to stop the thought-feeling-behavior patterns that keep you stuck. That said, it'll be exponentially easier to heal if you aren't actively communicating with your ex because contact with them makes your symptoms worse—something we'll explore in more detail in the next chapter.

So, if you're really in the dark depths of despair, you may be very committed to letting go of your ex because you'll do just about anything to feel better. Often, hitting rock bottom is a motivator for change (Kirouac and Witkiewitz 2017; Norcross, Krebs, and Prochaska 2011). If you just broke up, however, you may not want to leave your ex behind just yet. Or you may not be fully committed to doing the daily work it's going to take to heal and move on without them. Even if you and your ex parted ways long ago, you might be ambivalent about a life that doesn't include their shadow waiting for you in the background.

My goal for you—and hopefully your goal for yourself—is that you'll overcome your addiction to your ex. To reduce the obsessive thinking, cravings, emotional distress, and unhelpful behaviors so you can create the next phase of your life—one that brings you joy, fulfillment, and personal empowerment. Using the CBT skills in this book, you can actively stop the harmful symptoms that make you miserable. You can learn to let go of your ex and release the heavy heartache of this breakup. As you do, the energy you've spent suffering can be reinvested in your future—to growing, exploring, and experimenting with the next phase of your life. So, let's prepare you to practice the skills in this book, especially as you encounter rough patches that may lie ahead.

EXERCISE: Staying Committed to Letting Go

I want you to write a motivational statement to remind yourself why you're doing this work. Start by describing your most distressing symptoms; referring back to the Exaholic Assessment Questionnaire may help you to describe exactly how you're suffering. Then outline the costs of changing and not changing. What'll be most difficult for you about letting go of your ex? What would be most difficult about staying the same? Finally, describe exactly how you want to change and your commitment to letting go of your ex, along with some positive affirmations to keep you motivated along the way.

To get you started, take a look at the motivational statement that Maria wrote in her journal.

Right now, I'm in tremendous pain. I scored an 89 on the Exaholic Assessment Questionnaire, which means I'm experiencing strong symptoms that are negatively affecting my well-being. I am obsessively thinking about John, crave his attention, am emotionally distraught, and act in ways that ultimately make me feel worse. If I change, I'll have to accept that we're broken up and that I need to move on without him. I'll need to stop communicating and sleeping with him. I may even need to get off social media for a while. All of that's going to be very hard. But, if I don't change, the cost is that I'm going to stay stuck in this hellish reality. I'll remain completely obsessed with him—feeling lost and hopeless—at the expense of enjoying my life. So, I'm committed to practicing the skills in this book. I want to spend less time thinking about him. I want to feel better about who I am as a person. I want to take my power back by investing my energy in my future instead of dwelling in the past. I want to have a family, and that isn't going to happen with John. So, I'm actively committed to letting him go and moving on without him.

After you've written a statement that feels authentic to you, read it anytime you need to remind yourself why you're doing this work. You can even make copies and post them in places you see regularly—on the back of your closet door, on the bathroom mirror, in your purse or wallet, on your phone, or in the car. Read your statement to stay on track during your toughest moments.

Moving Forward

Your recovery from this breakup starts with one big choice: to let go of your ex and help yourself heal by picking up this book. But that's just the beginning of your journey. Every day you'll need to do something differently to resist the urges to fall back into old patterns because it's not actually one large choice that changes you: *it's the compounding effect of the thousands of seemingly small choices you make throughout the day to help yourself heal that ultimately sets you free.* Creating the next chapter of your life without the weight of this breakup pulling you down starts with writing one letter on the blank page of your future. Before you know it, you'll have composed a word, then a sentence, and eventually a paragraph. As you practice the CBT skills in this book and respond to your breakup differently, your choices will organically compose the next phase of your life. You'll undoubtedly make mistakes along the way, and that's okay! Don't give up or lose hope if you have moments of weakness because your self-promoting efforts will multiply over time. Soon, you'll be the author of your next great adventure.

In the next chapter, we'll start with the first task to making this new life a reality: dealing with your most difficult symptoms. You'll learn about the exaholic cycle of addiction and how the desire to be close to your ex fuels your heartache. Then you'll practice a host of CBT skills designed to interrupt the cycle itself and help you feel better.

CHAPTER 2

Relieving Your Most Difficult Symptoms

The worst part of this breakup is that I can't stop thinking about my ex. It's been two weeks since I heard from him and I literally think about him all the time. The more I think about him, the more I want to be with him. I even drove past his house today to see if his car was there. How pathetic is that?! I feel like such a loser.

Every time I see her, I feel a little better—even if we fight. At least I know she cares and I feel alive again for a minute. But after she leaves, my anxiety kicks in. I feel more and more panicked and I'm back where I started, trying to see her again. It's like I'm in a never-ending cycle of torture. I can't live with her and I can't live without her.

I know that trying to get my ex back is only bringing me more heartache. Intellectually, I know that it's over. And it should be—we're not good together. So, why can't I stop reaching out? Why do I cling to hope? Why do I care so much? I don't even like him right now! I don't know how I got here or how to move on.

As is true for the exaholics above, your internal world is probably laser-focused on your ex right now—and it's making you miserable. I want you to know that I have tremendous respect for anyone who acknowledges that they're struggling with something and actively takes steps to change. That's really the best we can do as humans. When we encounter difficult experiences in life, we either let them break us or we use them to learn about ourselves, evolve, and move forward. You're clearly choosing the latter, so give yourself credit for the efforts you're already making to heal from this breakup.

Now that you've committed to letting go of your ex and moving on, the next priority is to get you some relief from your symptoms. You already learned that when you broke up, the pleasure center in an old part of your brain stopped pumping you full of feel-good love chemicals, thrusting you into a state of withdrawal (Bobby 2015; Fisher 2016; Fisher et al. 2002). These jarring biological shifts coincided with a complete lifestyle renovation: your routines, mutual friends, inside jokes, moments of intimate closeness, and even home may have changed in the blink of an eye. You may have even lived together, had children, or been married. Now you're left trying to heal the pain of the past while starting a new life without your ex in it. As painful as that is to live through, understanding how your symptoms function in your life is the best way to stop them. So, we're going to explore your thought-feeling-behavior patterns in more detail.

Understanding the Exaholic Cycle

Although it may seem like your symptoms are independent, isolated experiences that function on their own, they actually interact with each other. When you're obsessively thinking about your ex, you'll crave them more, have stronger emotional reactions, and be more likely to act in ways that ultimately hurt you. Think of your symptoms as part of an addictive exaholic cycle driven by the desire for *contact and closeness with your ex*. It may sound strange that wanting to feel close to your ex is fueling your symptoms given that you've broken up, so let's unpack that further.

As you know all too well, going through an exaholic breakup is heartwrenching. When you're mired in hurt and pain, you search for ways to feel better. And, as strange as it sounds, contact with your ex temporarily relieves your suffering because it's like using a drug again (Fisher et al. 2016). When you're around your ex, your brain gives you a hit of feel-good chemicals that momentarily makes you feel better. Even if you're fighting, you'll probably feel some relief! In addition, your symptoms simply aren't as strong in the presence of your ex; you aren't pining after them, obsessively thinking about them, or craving them in the same way because they're with you! In psychological terms, having contact with your ex *positively reinforces*, or strengthens, your desire for future contact by making you feel better in the moment (J. S. Beck 2021).

The problem with being around your ex is that you'll feel increasingly worse *after the contact ends*. As shown in figure 1, you'll feel a little better during and immediately after doing something that makes you feel close to your ex—after using your drug, so to speak. But as the fleeting closeness fades, your exaholic symptoms—the obsessive thinking, cravings to see them, emotional distress and reactivity, and desire to act in harmful compulsive and impulsive ways—come flooding back and often escalate until you make contact again. This pattern is especially damaging if your relationship is really over, because you'll yearn for contact and closeness even though there's little realistic hope that you'll get back together.

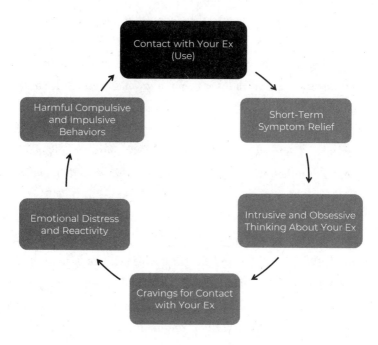

Figure 1: The exaholic cycle of love addiction.

It's always easier to see the exaholic cycle in other people than in ourselves, so let's consider another example. Deion was in a state of exaholic despair after he learned that his wife, Imani, was having an affair. The moment he walked into my office it was clear that Deion was full of conflicted resentment. Through tears and tensed jaw, he described stumbling upon a sexually explicit chat between Imani and another man. After breaking into her email account, Deion found more detailed information about his wife's affair: their favorite rendezvous hotels, dates of romantic dinners together, and highly provocative sexual dialogue. When Deion confronted Imani, she told him that he didn't make her feel special anymore and she had met someone who appreciates her. A huge fight ensued—complete with lots of name-calling, blaming, and yelling—and Imani moved out. Deion described his symptoms like this:

I was so furious when Imani left, but I also desperately wanted to understand why she cheated. At first, I emailed and texted her a lot—sometimes telling her how much I loved her and other times calling her vile names. I was all over the place. After a month or so, Imani told me she wanted space because I was acting so crazy, which made me feel worse. I mean, it was her fault I was in this position in the first place! One day when she wouldn't respond to my messages, I drove to her office and yelled at her in front of her coworkers. In the moment, I felt better. I told myself that she deserved to be humiliated just like I had been when I learned she had cheated. But, of course, it only made things worse. After that, Imani said I had become abusive and officially filed for divorce.

Now, I can't stop thinking about her—our life together, her affair, what went wrong. We vowed to be together forever, to love each other, to be faithful. I walk around our place looking at the pictures of our once happy family thinking about how much I miss her. Or, at least I miss the person that she was. Sometimes I even crawl onto her side of the bed and spray her perfume around the house so it feels like she's there. Other times I think about her cheating and want to punish her for hurting me so much. I can't get the images of her in bed with this guy out of my mind and it's driving me nuts! Our kids still see her, of course, which makes it harder for me. I'm drinking a lot, distracted at work, and have stopped taking care of the house. I'm so conflicted inside. I don't know how to let her go.

Do you see the exaholic cycle operating in Deion's life? Imani's affair complicates Deion's story and makes his pattern of symptoms quite erratic and volatile. That said, cheating is common in romantic relationships and can make the symptoms of love addiction worse because being betrayed often affects our thinking and emotions in extremely negative ways (Bobby 2015; Mellody, Miller, and Miller 2003). So, let's try to assess his patterns together.

Since Imani left, Deion's become fixated on her and thinks about her almost all the time. The more he relives the painful details of their breakup in his own mind, the more he craves her. He desperately wants to talk to her, punish her for cheating, and perhaps try to reconcile. Deion's obsessive thinking and cravings make him highly emotionally reactive and lead him to act in harmful ways, like showing up at her work and yelling at her. When Deion makes actual physical contact with Imani, he feels temporarily better. But Imani doesn't want to be around him, in part because his behavior is so unpredictable. So, he tries to feel close to her in other ways, like sleeping on her side of the bed, smelling her perfume, and looking at old family photos. After the closeness fades and reality sets in again, however, the exaholic cycle restarts: Deion thinks about her more, craves contact, feels emotionally gutted, and acts in ways that ultimately harm him and their relationship.

These intensely painful symptoms have dramatically influenced Deion's well-being. He's not taking care of his house, drinking too much, and struggling to focus at work. And while he knows Imani's cheating caused him tremendous heartache—as it generally does for anyone who's experienced it—his symptoms of love addiction thwart his ability to accept their breakup and move on without her. Ultimately, his addiction to Imani and fixation on her cheating keep him stuck in the miserable exaholic cycle.

Do you see the exaholic cycle in your relationship with your ex? Do you feel slightly better if you see them or hear from them, only to feel worse after the contact ends? Can you see how your symptoms interact and fuel each other? Becoming more aware of how the cycle functions in your life is critical to stopping your symptoms, so you're now going to learn how to do that more systematically.

EXERCISE: Monitoring Your Symptoms

One of the best ways to understand your pattern of symptoms is to use a self-monitoring log (A. T. Beck 1976; A. T. Beck et al. 1979; Ellis and Harper 1997; Tolin 2016). I can't emphasize enough how important this tool is because it serves as the foundation for every other CBT skill you'll learn in this book. Not only will completing daily logs help you track your symptoms and progress over time, but they will make it obvious where you need to intervene in the cycle itself to feel better.

You can create your own log in your journal or download a copy of my version, available at this book's website: http://www. newharbinger.com/50379. Starting now, as soon as you notice yourself having a symptom—an obsessive thought, a craving to reach out, a strong emotional reaction, or a desire to act in an unhealthy way—*pause*. In your log write down the *date*, *day*, and *time*. As is done in many 12-step programs (Alcoholics Anonymous World Services, Inc. 2003), also record the *number of days that have passed since you initiated contact with your ex*. If you must be in touch with your ex—because you have children, work together, are in a legal dispute, or have a unique situation that requires communication— then track the number of days that have passed since you initiated *unplanned* or *problematic contact* that wasn't necessary or scheduled in advance.

Next, describe the *situation:* What's going on in your life right now that's leading to your symptoms? Try to describe your surroundings in the most objective way possible, focusing on the facts without interpreting or reacting to them. Then record your *automatic thoughts:* the specific thoughts that're racing through your mind in response to the situation. Don't edit them; simply write down exactly what you're thinking. Finally, describe the specific *symptoms* you're experiencing and rate your *level of distress* at this exact moment on a scale from 1 (not at all distressed) to 10 (completely distressed).

After recording the situation and your automatic thoughts, symptoms, and level of distress, *pause again*, because it's time to take action. Instead of reacting to the situation as you have in the past, you're going to do a *self-care intervention:* do something to stop your symptoms that doesn't harm you in the long run. Over the course of this book you'll learn numerous CBT skills designed to help you do just that. For now, your goal is to help yourself feel better in healthy ways that lead you to avoid contact with your ex. Reading the motivational statement you created in chapter 1 is a great start. You could also go for a ten-minute walk, take a shower, brush your teeth, cuddle with your pet, or text a friend. Whatever you try, record it in your log as your self-care intervention and note its *effect on your symptoms* immediately after you do it. Specifically, describe how your level of overall distress, specific symptoms, or general sense of well-being shifted because of your self-care efforts.

Learning to use your log takes some practice, so let's run through some situations you may encounter together. Imagine you wake up one morning and, as you reach for your phone, you feel an overwhelming urge to send a message to your ex. As soon as you become aware of your craving, pause and fill out your log. Your entry might look something like this:

July 1. Thursday. 6:15 a.m.   Day 3 no contact.

Situation: I just woke up and grabbed my phone.

Automatic thoughts: I want to text my ex. We used to send messages every morning. I don't want our relationship to be over. I miss him so much!

Symptoms: I'm desperate to reach out—my cravings are strong. I feel sad and lonely.

Level of distress: 7.

Self-care intervention: I'm going to take a shower, make a cup of coffee, and read my motivational statement to keep myself from texting him.

Effect on symptoms: My cravings weakened and my overall distress went down to a 5 after my self-care efforts.

Here's another example. You're at work and a mutual friend invites you to a party tonight. You immediately feel anxious and a little excited. As soon as you become aware of your feelings, you pause and write in your log:

January 9. Friday. 3:00 p.m.   Day 12 no contact.

Situation: Our friend is having a party tonight.

Automatic thoughts: My ex might be there, which makes me want to go. But it also makes me think I shouldn't go. She may not even want to see me.

Symptoms: I feel excited and anxious. My thoughts are racing.

Level of distress: 6.

Self-care intervention: I know it's not good for me to see my ex right now. I'm calling a friend to make other plans tonight because I'll need some support!

Effect on symptoms: My distress is now a 4. Planning for tonight helped me feel more in control of my symptoms.

Let's consider one final example. It's late at night and you've been especially emotional all day. You are home alone, have had a couple glasses of wine, and see an advertisement for a TV series you used to watch with your ex. In an impulsive moment, you text them a picture of the upcoming season with the message, "Wish you were here." Immediately after sending the text you start to panic. You pause and make an entry in your log:

August 18. Sunday. 11:00 p.m.   Day 0 no contact.

Situation: I just saw an ad for our favorite show and texted my ex.

Automatic thoughts: I shouldn't have texted! I look desperate. I hope he responds. I want him to come over. I ruined my streak of not initiating contact. I'm such a disaster!

Symptoms: I feel incredibly anxious. My thoughts are racing. I feel out of control and impulsive. I want to guzzle the rest of this wine to distract myself. I'm going to be looking at my phone all night to see if he responds.

Level of distress: 10.

Self-care intervention: I'm going to put away the bottle, take a bath, and go to sleep. I'm turning off my phone so that I can't text my ex again tonight. It's going to be hard, but I'll read my motivational statement to remind myself why I'm doing this.

Effect on symptoms: My distress is still high, but my cravings are weaker and I'm managing my behavior more effectively.

As shown in the examples above, record your symptoms in your log at least twice a day, every day, starting today. In fact, I want you to use your log as often as possible, because the more information you gather the easier it'll be to see your patterns and stop your symptoms before they escalate (J. S. Beck 2021). Just filling it out often helps you make healthier choices in the moment! Even if you don't always feel better immediately after doing a self-care intervention, remember that it's choosing to respond to your symptoms in self-promoting ways repeatedly throughout the day that ultimately heals you over time.

As you practice recording your experiences in your log and experiment with new self-care interventions, it'll be important to utilize CBT skills to stop the exaholic cycle itself, so let's arm you with some. We're going to start by tackling the first—and perhaps most difficult—change you'll want to make: cutting off contact with your ex.

Cutting Off Contact with Your Ex

Cutting off contact with your ex probably sounds like an incredibly hard task—because it is! In fact, you'll probably feel temporarily worse when you do. In CBT terms, we call this an *extinction burst*: as you break the connection between yourself and your ex, you'll feel a greater urge to be around them. It doesn't feel good to experience an extinction burst, but you need to unlearn the pleasure you associate with your ex and relearn ways to feel good without them. It will be much easier to move on after the association between your ex and pleasure weakens (Tolin 2016).

Ideally, you want to stop initiating all communication with your ex because closeness fuels your exaholic cycle! Cutting off contact doesn't mean your ex will be out of your life forever: it will become clear to you over time whether you're capable of having them in your life in a healthy way (Bobby 2015; Halpern-Meekin et al. 2013). For now, it will be easier to address your symptoms if you aren't actively communicating with your ex. If you can't cut off contact completely, or if your ex continues to communicate with you, your goal is to reduce contact as much as possible and to set clear expectations about when and how you'll interact (we'll practice doing this in the "Setting Healthy Boundaries" section in chapter 3).

Cutting off contact with your ex also means pausing all behaviors aimed at making you feel connected or close to them. This includes things like stopping yourself from searching for information about them online, rereading old emails or texts, and inspecting old photos. In addition, it's important to remove items from your physical space that remind you of your ex, like meaningful gifts they gave you and their toothbrush.

EXERCISE: Minimizing Contact with Your Ex

Take a few minutes to consider everything you do to feel close to your ex, including things like calling them, asking mutual friends about them, wearing their old T-shirt, trying to run into them at their favorite coffee shop, or even spraying their perfume around the house like Deion did. Then compose a "reduce contact list" of things you can do to stop yourself from feeling close to them. Keep in mind that you don't have to commit to these things forever. For now, however, I strongly recommend that you strive to do the following:

- Stop initiating unplanned contact with your ex: no emailing, texting, or calling.

- Stop trying to get information about your ex online or from friends.

- Stop sexual interactions with your ex.

- Reduce social media use or block your ex there (at least temporarily).

- Remove all photos, gifts, letters, and reminders of your ex from your personal space (store them if you don't want to throw them away).

- Stop trying to run into your ex, such as by going to their hangouts or following them.

- Give away or mail your ex's stuff back to them.

- Consider taking time away from mutual friends (at least temporarily).

After you have a solid list, it's time to take action. This is probably going to be really hard, so be gentle with yourself and do the best you can. Start with tasks that seem easier and work up to the harder ones, but commit to doing all of them. Record your efforts in your log as self-care interventions.

As you reduce physical contact and closeness with your ex, you'll also need to stop feeling close to them through your thoughts. That's much easier said than done, so let's practice some ways to manage your thinking.

Managing Your Thoughts

You already know that thinking about your ex is one of the most distressing symptoms of an exaholic breakup. What's more, when you're thinking about them you're actually making contact with them in your own mind. They're consuming space in your head even though they aren't actively your partner anymore! The more you think about them, the more you'll crave them, feel emotionally distressed, and want to act in ways that ultimately hurt you. So, you want to set limits on how much time and energy you're willing to spend thinking about your ex.

Although it may sound strange, you don't want to avoid thinking about your ex completely; avoiding emotions associated with difficult life experiences puts you at risk for developing other potentially harmful symptoms later (J. S. Beck 2021; Heshmati, Zemestani, and Vujanovic 2021; Tolin 2016). But you don't want intrusive and obsessive thoughts about your ex dominating your mind anymore. The key is to find a balance between thinking about your ex in a productive way and not thinking about them when you don't want to be.

A good way to do this is to schedule a dedicated *rumination time* (Clark 2020) and to practice *thought-stopping* (Davis, Eshelman, and McKay 1988). During your scheduled rumination time, your only job is to think about your ex and your breakup. You can scream, cry, argue with your ex in a role-playing way, verbally say everything you wish you could tell them, draw, or journal—whatever gets the preoccupying thoughts out of your head. When the time's up, you're done thinking about your ex until the next scheduled rumination time. To do that, you're going to practice thought-stopping:

when you notice intrusive, obsessive, or generally unwanted thoughts about your ex, say the word *stop* to yourself; you can yell it out loud if you're alone! Then close your eyes and visualize a large red stop sign. Imagine a beautiful, peaceful place that makes you feel safe, and go there in your mind. In this pleasant space, any thoughts or images of your ex are met with the word "stop" and pushed away, while your peaceful beach scene or tranquil golden sunset captures your attention. Remind yourself that you can think about your ex again during the next rumination time, but not before. Practice thought-stopping for five-to-ten-minute increments any time you need to shift your thoughts away from your ex.

EXERCISE: Stopping Obsessive Thinking

Establish a rumination time devoted to thinking only about your ex. Start by scheduling fifteen minutes three times a day. For many people the best times are when they wake up in the morning, around lunch, and when they get home at night. When the time for a scheduled session arrives, set a timer and focus only on your ex and your breakup. You may soon realize that this is too much or not enough time for you, so experiment with what works best, but don't give yourself more than twenty minutes per session.

After you finish, it's time to practice thought-stopping. Whenever upsetting images or intrusive thoughts of your ex enter your mind over the course of the day, say "stop" and focus on a relaxing, soothing image instead. As you get better at doing this over time, you can replace "stop" with the word "calm" and enjoy this exercise as a peaceful visualization. Anytime you practice these skills, add them to your log as self-care interventions and record how they affect your symptoms.

Like all the skills in this book, effectively using rumination time and thought-stopping takes practice, but it gets easier over time. As you gain some control over when and how much you think about your ex, you'll also want to manage your urges to reach out. We're going to tackle your cravings next.

Overcoming Your Cravings

In moments of intense craving, you'll feel desperate urges to communicate and reconnect with your ex. It may feel like seeing your ex is the only thing that can give you relief, that your craving's going to escalate until you give in to it (National Institute on Drug Abuse 2020). Yet the truth is that your craving will diminish over time if you don't react to it. It's inevitable because the intensity of a craving can't stay at high levels forever! So, you can learn to *ride out* your cravings, letting yourself experience whatever authentic emotions emerge in the process until the urge subsides (Ashe, Newman, and Wilson 2015).

Let's consider an example to see what riding out cravings looks like in action. It's a Friday night and you're finishing dinner with a friend after work. As you get up to leave, an overwhelming urge to stop by your ex's place on your way home comes over you. You notice your reaction, pause, and complete your log as soon as possible.

August 5. Thursday. 8:00 p.m.   Day 14 no contact.

Situation: I'm just leaving dinner with a friend.

Automatic thoughts: I want to go to my ex's place on my way home. I need to see him.

Symptoms: I have an overwhelming craving; it's so strong I can barely stand it.

Level of distress: 9.

Self-care intervention: I haven't contacted him for fourteen days and I don't want to make my symptoms worse! So, I'm going home to practice riding out the craving.

Effect on symptoms: My cravings are weaker and my distress level went down to a 5. I'm going to thank myself in the morning for not going to my ex's tonight!

In moments of intense cravings like this, you'll need to make a choice not to act on them. The more you ride them out, the more you'll see that cravings are temporary; they'll eventually subside if you don't give in to them. Even more importantly, you'll see that you're stronger than you may think! You can survive your urges and control your symptoms by changing your responses to them, which builds your self-esteem, self-efficacy, grit, and resilience over time (O'Sullivan et al. 2019).

EXERCISE: Riding Out Your Cravings

No matter how strong your urge to contact your ex feels, it'll eventually pass. Practicing riding out your cravings can help you avoid acting on them. When you have a strong urge to reach out to your ex, note your level of distress in your log and set a timer for ten minutes. Now, just sit and don't give in to the craving. If you're feeling particularly bad, use another CBT skill—like reading your motivational statement and thought-stopping—to get through it. It'll be uncomfortable not acting on your urge, but you can live through it. When the time's up, reevaluate how strong the craving is; if it's still high, continue to ride out your craving in ten-minute intervals until it subsides enough that you can move on with your day. When you're done, record it as a self-care intervention in your log and write down how your symptoms shifted.

As you practice reducing contact, thought-stopping, rumination time, and riding out your cravings, you're going to feel uncomfortable. None of us likes that because it's so unpleasant, but discomfort is inevitable right now. So, learning to cope with your emotional distress in healthier ways is essential.

Coping with Distressing Emotions

Often in life we find ourselves in situations we don't want to be in or can't control. You can't control your ex. You can't control many things about this breakup. You don't want to feel addicted to your ex, but you are and you're emotionally struggling because of it.

Radical acceptance (Ellis and Harper 1997; Linehan 2014) will help you cope with the most distressing emotions related to your breakup. Feeling negative emotions isn't bad. These emotions are providing you with information, and feeling them is a natural part of the human experience when something happens that we don't like or want. Radical acceptance is telling yourself the truth about the situation you're in—that your relationship is over, at least for today—and dealing with the feelings associated with that reality. When you're struggling to let go of your ex, you may try to deceive yourself by thinking things like *I can't live without them* or *I have to make them want me again. I can fix this.* Those thoughts will be reflected in your behaviors and feelings as you try to entice your ex back or live in a fantasy that's ultimately untrue. A more honest response to your breakup may be something like *I'm very sad that my ex and I broke up. I wish we were still together. But we're not, so I'm going to make choices that reflect that reality.* Letting yourself feel authentic emotion associated with your breakup instead of staying fixated on how your relationship used to be or could be in the future will help you move on.

You might find radical acceptance very hard at first, and that's totally understandable. You're exposing yourself to the raw reality of your situation and asking yourself to see and accept it exactly as it is. When you tell yourself the truth and feel authentic emotion as a result, you'll become less reactive to the truth over time because it'll have less power over you. (You'll spend a lot of time learning to evaluate the accuracy of your thoughts and beliefs in part 2 of this book, and you're going to become very skilled at it over time.)

EXERCISE: Practicing Radical Acceptance

Take a moment to practice radical acceptance by acknowledging that your relationship is over—that you've lost a person, a dream, and a lifestyle that meant a great deal to you. Let yourself feel any emotions that emerge from this reality. Sit with them and do nothing to stop them. Just be there. Let yourself feel the anger, sadness, bitterness, hurt, or fear. Anytime you notice yourself slipping back into untrue fantasies about your relationship by reliving the past, wishing you were together again, or trying to find ways to change your ex, pause and shift back to radically accepting the truth that you're not currently together. Doing this after a scheduled rumination time can be particularly helpful: after deliberately thinking about your ex and expressing your internal angst, end your rumination time by reminding yourself in a raw but self-affirming way that your relationship's over. Record your efforts in your log as a self-care intervention.

As you tackle your thinking, cravings, and emotional distress, it's time to address your harmful behaviors. As you might recall, these attempts to help yourself feel closer to your ex or to distract yourself from the pain of this breakup make you feel slightly better in the moment, but they damage your well-being over time and need to stop.

Stopping Harmful Behaviors

During an exaholic breakup, your behaviors tend to be either compulsive or impulsive attempts to cope with your pain (Koob and Volkow 2010). When you act *compulsively*, you're doing something repetitively and continually (Luigjes et al. 2019). These behaviors look habitual, like refreshing your email or checking your phone every few minutes to see whether you got a message from your ex. Conversely, when you act *impulsively*, you're acting without thinking about the potential consequences of your behavior

(Bakshani 2014). For example, when feeling an unbearable craving you may jump in your car on a whim and show up at your ex's house or go on an unplanned shopping spree and spend far more money than you can afford to.

Compulsive and impulsive behaviors make you feel better for a fleeting moment, which is why we do them, but they also fuel your other symptoms and lead to a host of negative consequences. Compulsive behaviors occupy your time and energy in a preoccupying, repetitive way, whereas impulsive behaviors are usually things you wouldn't have done had you stopped to consider the consequences of your actions before you did them. Looking back, for example, you wouldn't have drunk-dialed your ex from a bar late at night had you thought about how bad you'd feel in the morning. Similarly, odds are you wouldn't have gone on that shopping spree had you considered how much money you were going to spend on things you don't really want.

The key to managing harmful behaviors is to consider the consequences *before* you do them. Let's look at some examples together. Imagine that you see this pattern from your completed logs: when you're feeling especially anxious you compulsively check your phone to see if your ex texted you. The primary pro (or positive effect) of engaging in this behavior is that you feel short-term relief from your symptoms—the obsessive thinking, cravings, and distressing emotions. Yet the primary cons (or negative effects) of this behavior are massive: it keeps you fixated on your ex, wastes large amounts of your time and energy, fuels your exaholic cycle, and makes you feel worse about yourself over time. So, as soon as you become aware that you're compulsively checking your phone, pause and record your experience in your log:

August 27. Friday. 5:00 p.m.   Day 34 no contact.

Situation: I'm feeling anxious. I've been checking my phone all day to see if my ex texted me.

Automatic thoughts: She doesn't care about me anymore. Why can't I let her go! The weekend's coming and I still haven't heard from her.

Symptoms: I'm getting more and more emotionally upset and physically sick to my stomach. The worse I feel the more I want her.

Level of distress: 8.

Self-care intervention: I'm considering the consequences: If I keep checking my phone or text her, I'll feel slightly better for a moment but far worse in the long run because it keeps me fixated on her! So, I'm putting down my phone and practicing radical acceptance: we're broken up and I'm committed to moving on without her.

Effect on symptoms: I'm feeling more confident. My distress is down to a 5.

Here's another example. Let's say that when you're most desperate to feel close to your ex you send a sexy picture of yourself. The primary pros of this behavior are that you may receive positive feedback, and the contact will give you short-term relief from your symptoms. You may even entice your ex to come over for a hot hookup. The primary cons, however, are many: you may spend hours overanalyzing every detail of your message, feel embarrassed because your text makes you look desperate for your ex's attention, or feel even more upset if your ex doesn't respond. Plus, of course, this behavior fuels your exaholic cycle over time. So, as soon as you become aware that you want to send a photo, pause and complete your log:

September 1. Wednesday. 9:00 p.m.   Day 12 no contact.

Situation: I'm really struggling emotionally. I want to send a sexy picture to my ex.

Automatic thoughts: I want his attention! Maybe if he sees how good I look he'll want me again. I want some acknowledgment—anything to validate that he still cares! Maybe I can find a date to distract myself tonight. Then I can post a picture of us online to get my ex's attention.

Symptoms: I'm feeling completely panicked and desperate for contact.

Level of distress: 9.5.

Self-care intervention: I'm considering the consequences: If I send a photo, he may say that I look hot or even come over. But where does that leave me?! We'll still be broken up. Plus, he may not even answer, which would make me feel more rejected than I already do. And dating another guy just to make my ex jealous is a terrible idea. So, I'm not sending the picture. I'm going to call a friend instead.

Effect on symptoms: My distress decreased to a 6 after I decided not to send the picture. I know it's the right choice. I'm proud of myself for not giving in to my urges.

Considering the consequences of your behaviors before you act will help you intervene in your exaholic cycle before it gets worse. It'll also save you from making choices you ultimately regret.

EXERCISE: Considering the Consequences

Identify the behaviors you do to feel close to your ex or to distract yourself from your pain. You can use your completed self-monitoring logs to find common examples. Then, as we did above, consider the consequences of engaging in each behavior by describing the primary pros and cons of each in your journal. As you reflect on the ways you've acted that left you feeling terrible—we've all been there—use them to remind yourself of why you're not going to do them again in the future. The next time you want to act in that same harmful way, pause, remember the longer-term negative consequences of that behavior, and choose a healthier response. Record your efforts in your log as a self-care intervention.

Moving Forward

As you learn to assess and track the exaholic cycle in your life using your self-monitoring log, your harmful thought-feeling-behavior patterns will become more obvious. As they do, you'll see how you're unintentionally making your symptoms worse and where you can intervene to stop them from snowballing. Practicing the CBT skills you're learning here—using your log, cutting off contact, scheduling rumination time, practicing thought-stopping, riding out cravings, and considering the consequences before you act—will not only reduce your symptoms over time but build your self-confidence. You'll see that you can help yourself by making more self-affirming choices in response to difficult situations you encounter. Don't be hard on yourself if you struggle or make a mistake; this is all new and it takes practice! Read your motivational statement to remind yourself that you're committed to using these skills even when it's hard, because you want to let go of your ex and create a fulfilling future.

In the next chapter, we're going to explore situational factors—called "triggers"—that make your symptoms worse, and plan for them. We're also going to find new ways to help you feel good without your ex! This includes setting healthier boundaries, getting more social support, meeting your physical health needs, and perhaps even finding a skilled therapist to help you along the way.

CHAPTER 3

Managing Triggers and Increasing Self-Care

I'm on day twenty-seven of not initiating contact. As I use my self-monitoring log, I see that trying to get information about my ex ultimately makes me feel worse. I need to stop focusing on him so I can build a new life. It's so painful, but I know that I need to do it.

I'm aware that when I walk past the park on my way home from work, I'm going to think of her. When I see our old coffee spot, my mind starts racing with memories and the things I so desperately want to say. So, now, I plan for it. I practice thought-stopping before I even get to the park. Or, if I'm having a really bad day, I walk another way home.

It's been forty-two days since I contacted my ex. Sometimes it's agony not to reach out, but I'm learning to ride out the cravings. My mind wants to let go and move on, but my heart can't seem to. So, I'll keep counting the days and practicing these skills until my heart catches up to my head.

As is evident in the quotes above, changing the thought-feeling-behavior patterns that revolve around your ex is incredibly hard. Up until very recently, you may not have even been aware that your symptoms functioned in an addictive exaholic cycle. You probably didn't see how feeling close to your ex—in person or in your own mind—makes your symptoms worse. Not only does contact make you think about them more, have stronger cravings, feel more emotionally distressed, and prone to act in ways that ultimately hurt you, but it also erodes your self-esteem over time. You may even have forgotten the fundamental truth that *you're just as valuable as a single person as you were when you were with your ex.*

The changes you're trying to make are also tough because you're responding to your breakup in a totally different way. That takes practice, commitment, and a lot of deliberate effort. Now when you catch yourself obsessively thinking about your ex, you pause and practice thought-stopping. When you notice yourself looking at old texts, you pause and remember that to move on you need to stop feeling close to your ex in your own mind. When you want to act in compulsive or impulsive ways, you pause and consider the consequences before you do something you might regret. As you practice, you'll see that you can change your exaholic symptoms by responding to them differently. That's where your true power lies: although you can't control your ex or make this breakup go away, *you can make choices that help you feel better.* You can take your power back by choosing to put your energy into healing instead of staying mired in past pain.

As you continue to track your symptoms in your log and practice new self-care interventions, you'll get better at predicting situations that'll be hardest for you. This helps you to plan for them and intervene before they cause your symptoms to flare. In this chapter, we're going to identify your triggers and increase your self-care so you can find some enjoyment in life again. Let's get started.

Understanding and Managing Your Triggers

Have you noticed that some situations automatically remind you of your ex and immediately make your symptoms worse? Maybe you struggle more on Tuesdays after work because it was half-off wine night at your local bistro. Maybe it's seeing a golden retriever at the park because that was your ex's favorite dog. Maybe it's July 4th weekend because that's when you always went on vacation together. Maybe it's driving by the hotel where your ex had an affair. Maybe it's noticing a certain sports team is playing. Maybe it's going to yoga class. Maybe it's when you feel extra stressed at work because your ex always knew exactly what to say to make you feel better when you were upset.

These situations or events that remind you of your ex and make you want to contact them are called *triggers* (Asensio, Hernández-Rabaza, and Orón Semper 2020; Starcke et al. 2018; von Hammerstein et al. 2020). Triggers are often stimuli in the outside world: seeing people that remind you of your ex, activities you used to do together, holidays, smells, or traditions you shared. Triggers can also be the thoughts, feelings, and sensations in your mind and body that make you think about your ex. For example, your ex may immediately pop into your head when you're feeling more emotional than usual, having health issues, being sexually active with another person, or even just feeling tired. The problem with triggers is that when you encounter them, your symptoms are likely to erupt immediately. And the worse you feel in the moment you encounter the trigger, the more you're going to want to reach out to your ex, because triggers make you want to "use" whatever substance or behavior you feel addicted to (von Hammerstein et al. 2020).

Some triggers—many of which you've already made efforts to change—are troublesome for anyone going through a difficult breakup. Looking at old pictures, walking by your ex's home, trying to learn who your ex is dating now, or picturing them having sex with another lover often triggers strong symptoms. But many of your triggers will be very specific to you. The more aware you are of them, the better able you are to plan your response so they don't send you further into the exaholic cycle.

As we begin to identify your triggers, let's consider Mei's story. Mei started therapy shortly after divorcing her husband, Mohammed. Although she intellectually believed that ending her marriage was the right choice for her and their two children, Mei couldn't seem to move on. She was consumed by memories of happier times early in her marriage. When pressed about why she left, Mei said that Mohammed drank too much, was narcissistic, and refused to go to therapy. The final blow came when Mohammed missed an important family event after a late-night bender. Although Mei initiated their divorce, she had the classic symptoms of an exaholic: she doubted her decision to leave, focused only on the positive aspects of their former relationship, and felt extremely guilty for "breaking up their family." What's more, the fact that they had children together meant that Mei couldn't cut off contact completely.

As we worked together, some of Mei's most troublesome triggers became obvious. Let's look at three of her logs to practice identifying them. See if you can spot any triggers that made her symptoms worse.

September 16. Thursday. Midnight. Day 56 of no unplanned contact.

Situation: Mohammed is picking up the kids tomorrow.

Automatic thoughts: What's he doing with them? Is another woman going to be there? I wish we were still together.

Symptoms: I'm thinking obsessively about Mohammed and his time with the kids. I feel incredibly anxious. I feel physically ill and have no appetite.

Level of distress: 7.

Self-care intervention: I completed two sessions of rumination time and am actively practicing thought–stopping. I'm also using radical acceptance: I'm reminding myself that we're divorced and that I have no control over what Mohammed does now.

Effect on symptoms: After my self–care efforts, my emotional distress and physical symptoms improved to the degree that I was able to fall asleep.

September 18. Saturday. 11:30 a.m. Day 58 of no unplanned contact.

Situation: Mohammed has the kids. I'm home alone.

Automatic thoughts: We were so happy when we first got married. He can change. We can get back to the way it was. I gave up on our marriage too quickly. It's my fault we broke up.

Symptoms: My thoughts are racing! I feel sad, anxious, and depressed. I can't stop crying. I have a strong urge to drive to his place and beg him to take me back.

Level of distress: 10.

Self-care intervention: I'm reading my motivational statement over and over. I'm sitting with my feelings and considering the consequences of my choices before I act. I'm choosing not to drive over to his house. I'm riding out my cravings. I'm reaching to my skills instead of to Mohammad.

Effect on symptoms: I'm still very distressed, but I'm not acting on my urges. I'm not as panicky as I was before using my skills.

September 20. Monday. 6:30 a.m.   Day 60 of no unplanned contact.

Situation: I just woke up. Our kids are at home and asleep.

Automatic thoughts: What did they do over the weekend? Does he ever think about me? I'm so pathetic that I can't move on. At least the kids are home with me now.

Symptoms: I feel calmer than I did over the weekend, but I'm emotionally exhausted. I want to stop obsessing about him.

Level of distress: 5.

Self-care intervention: I'm using thought–stopping and practicing radical acceptance—Mohammed isn't the same man I married. We're better off divorced.

Effect on symptoms: I'm so grateful I got through the weekend without doing anything I would really regret now! My overall distress is down to a 4 and I feel stronger—I got through the weekend without giving in to my symptoms in unhealthy ways.

Do you see some of Mei's triggers in her logs? You may notice that being home alone on the weekend when Mohammed has the kids is a huge trigger for her. Starting with her first log on Thursday night—the day before Mohammed picked up the kids—Mei became incredibly anxious and obsessively thought about what they would be doing. After her kids left, she became more and more upset; her emotional distress skyrocketed, and her obsessive thinking about what they were doing led her to feel intense urges to contact him and reunite. Her exaholic cycle was on fire! On Monday, when the kids were home and she was no longer alone, her symptoms decreased. She still didn't feel great—she's dealing with a love-addicted breakup and struggling to accept their divorce—but she wasn't triggered in such an extreme way anymore. This pattern was very typical for Mei and happened every weekend Mohammed took the kids.

Do you see triggers in your life? Are there situations or circumstances that make it harder for you to resist your ex? To stop your triggers from fueling your exaholic cycle, you need to become aware of them so you can respond in a self-enhancing way. Let's explore your triggers now.

EXERCISE: Identifying and Planning for Triggers

I want you to create a trigger list of external situations and internal experiences that make you want to contact your ex more strongly. Looking at your self-monitoring logs and journal, can you see any patterns for when you seem to really struggle? Are there specific days or times that trigger you? Like Mei, many people struggle on weekends or on days when they have less structure in their schedule. People are also often triggered at night, when they would have been sleeping with their ex, or when they're home alone.

Next, I want you to scrutinize what you wrote in the "situation" column of your logs. Are there circumstances that repeatedly come up for you? For example, when you're around certain people? When you're tired? Drinking alcohol? Out with friends who are in relationships or married? Out late at night? Experiencing financial stress? Around your family? Add any such situational triggers to your list.

Finally, think about the larger picture of your relationship with your ex. Are there times when you want to contact them more that aren't obvious in your logs? Specific times of year? Holidays or events? Birthdays? What about hobbies, names, colors, cities, places, restaurants, or people? Write these things down.

Now that you've identified some of your primary triggers, I want you to *plan for them*. Next to each item on your trigger list, write something you can do to cope with it in a healthy way. For example, if you know that Saturday nights are especially hard, you can plan dinner with a friend, go to a 12-step meeting, take a yoga class, or schedule an extra rumination time that night. If you know you're easily triggered when you're out drinking or partying with friends, before you go commit to not contacting your ex. You might even want to tell your friends of your difficulty and ask them to help you through it. Ultimately, your goal is to become aware of situations that are triggering to you and practice responding in a way that helps you stay grounded without reaching out to your ex.

Some healthy ways you can help yourself cope with triggers include:

- Adding structure to your day. Schedule activities that make you feel good during times that are most triggering for you.

- Getting social support. Call a friend or family member you trust to process your experience.

- Doing something to promote your mental health. Go to a therapy session, support group meeting, spiritual center, or church service. Or read a book, like this one!

- Changing your environment—get out of your immediate space and go somewhere that's pleasant for you. Get a coffee, go for a walk outside, eat a meal at your favorite restaurant, or peruse the paintings at your local art museum.

- Doing something to change your body awareness. Get some exercise, eat a healthy snack, take a warm bath, brush your teeth, or chew gum—anything to change your physical sensations.

- Journaling about your thoughts, feelings, and experiences.

- Doing something to give back to your community. Helping others is mutually beneficial.

- Practicing any of the skills you're learning in this book: rumination time, thought-stopping, riding out your cravings, radical acceptance, considering the consequences of your behaviors, or reading your motivational statement.

Many of my suggestions for managing triggers are self-care interventions intended to improve your well-being, which is critical right now. In addition to removing things from your life that hurt you, you want to fill your life with positive, enjoyable, and meaningful experiences as you recover from this breakup. You can do that by setting healthier boundaries, increasing your social support, taking better care of your health, and maybe even finding a skilled therapist. So, let's start improving your self-care skills now.

Setting Healthy Boundaries

Although many people think that boundaries are rules telling others how to act, that isn't actually true. Boundaries are all about you! They establish expectations for how you want to be treated in relationships and what you're going to do if someone violates your principles (Cloud and Townsend 2000). Boundaries can be physical or sexual, reflecting how you want people to touch you (and not touch you). They can be emotional, establishing how you want people to talk to you, process feelings with you, and connect with you. They can be financial, reflecting who pays for what and when. They can be relational, reflecting what kinds of interactions you do and don't expect to have with family, friends, and lovers. Really, boundaries are your expectations about how you'll interact with others in all areas of your life. Establishing and communicating your boundaries—as well as following through with consequences when they're violated—keeps you safe in your relationships with others.

It's really important for me to emphasize that boundaries aren't about controlling other people or telling other people who to be (Cloud and Townsend 2017). They're also not about punishment, retribution, or resentfully getting payback when someone acts in a way that hurts you. We all have the freedom to live as we see fit—including your ex. Boundaries aren't about infringing on anyone else's autonomy. In fact, if you act in ways to try to control or manipulate others, you'll hurt yourself, them, and your relationship with them (Mellody, Miller, and Miller 2003). Instead, boundaries are about clearly articulating who you are, how you do and don't want to be treated, and what you'll do if someone treats you in a way that you don't like (Cloud and Townsend 2017).

Right now, it's very likely that your boundaries with your ex are unclear and confusing because the nature of your relationship has changed! When a relationship ends, boundaries often become skewed because the dynamics between you and your former lover shift (Cloud and Townsend 2000). When you're feeling strong and clearheaded, you may be able to respectfully communicate to your ex what is and is not okay with you. And in those moments, it's easier to hold yourself and your ex accountable if one of you violates a boundary. But when you're trapped in the exaholic cycle, you may feel so bad that you'll take any closeness to feel some relief from your symptoms—even if it isn't consistent with your values, the way you want to act, or the way you want your ex to treat you. Fights, late-night booty calls, or pleas to get back together out of desperation are common during exaholic breakups, and ultimately they leave you feeling terrible (Bobby 2015; Halpern-Meekin et al. 2013).

The biggest problem with not having clear or consistent boundaries is that it'll be much harder for you to change the patterns of your interactions with your ex. In psychological terms, behavior that doesn't elicit consistent consequences is being *intermittently reinforced*, meaning that if your responses aren't predictable or consistent, people won't know what to expect from you (Tolin 2016). If you welcome your ex back into your life on some days but reject them on others, for example, your ex won't really know what you want because you're sending mixed messages. That's not good for you or your relationships because people won't trust you—and you won't trust yourself. Trust requires that what you say and do are consistent. That you mean what you say and act accordingly in good faith with honest intentions. So, it's important to set clear boundaries with your ex *and* follow through with whatever consequences you put in place.

Given that your boundaries with your ex are likely messy right now, I encourage you to consider establishing these expectations.

Strive not to initiate unplanned contact. Hopefully you now really understand why it's critical to limit contact with your ex: contact with your ex fuels your exaholic cycle and makes your symptoms worse. You've already been practicing cutting off contact, but if your ex reached out to you or you reached out to them recently in a moment of weakness, reestablish this boundary of no unplanned contact for now.

If you can't cut off contact completely, you'll want to set clear expectations about how and when you'll communicate, and what you will and won't talk about. Your goals in communicating with your ex should be to review information that's necessary—like the kids' schedules, financial obligations, legal updates, work requirements, or travel plans—and to avoid intimate conversations that make you feel close to them. For now, I strongly recommend that you only communicate by email on a set schedule, like sending an update every Monday morning. Email is useful because you can take your time to carefully craft your message, ensuring its content and tone are respectfully clear before sending (Bobby 2015). Save texting and phone calls for emergencies because they're ripe for misunderstandings and emotional reactions that are much harder to resolve in the moment.

Pause sexually charged interactions. I encourage you not to have any kind of sexual interaction or romantic communication with your ex. Using sex as a tool to get attention from your ex has the potential to make you feel worse over time (Halpern-Meekin et al. 2013; Mellody, Miller, and Miller 2003), and sex and orgasms release hormones in your body that make you feel closer to them (Fisher 2016). This can lead you to be more attracted and attached to your ex, which makes it even harder for you to move on.

Pause friendship today. Someday you may be able to be friends with your ex, but not yet. Only time will tell whether you'll want to have a platonic relationship with them in the future or are capable of it. For now, keep your distance, because you need space to heal.

Pause trying to get back together. Today, you're broken up. So, by definition, something about your relationship isn't working for you, your ex, or both of you. For you to reunite in the future, something about your relationship will need to change. Until that happens, focus on yourself. If you and your ex decide you want to get back together, a good therapist may be able to help you work toward that goal (Mellody, Miller, and Miller 2003).

Moving on without your ex will be much easier if you have good, strong boundaries. If you've already cut off contact with them, congratulations! Keep counting the days. If you've been in contact with your ex—because you slipped or they contacted you—establishing clear boundaries will help you move on.

EXERCISE: Setting Your Boundaries

In your journal, compose a boundary statement to establish how you want to interact with your ex moving forward. Ultimately this statement is more for you than it is for your ex, so you may never share it with them. But, if you ever want to communicate your boundaries directly to your ex, you can use it to guide your interaction.

As if you were writing your ex a letter, start by describing how you want to interact with them. For most, this statement reflects the expectation that you aren't going to have any direct contact right now. Then describe what you'll do if contact is made. For example:

To heal and establish a new life for myself without you, I need space. Someday I may be able to communicate with you again, but I'm not ready for that today. So, I won't contact you anymore, and I'm asking you to do the same. If you reach out to me after today, I won't respond. I wish you the best.

If you can't cut off contact completely, like Mei, you'll want to communicate boundaries that include contact with your ex. To do that, craft a statement that articulates what you expect or want from your interactions, how you'll act, how you'd like them to act, and what you'll do if your boundaries are violated. For example, here's Mei's boundary statement for her ex-husband:

Dear Mohammed,

I want to find a productive way of communicating with you about our kids. My goal is to review the kids' schedules and any specific upcoming events—like travel or days off school—to ensure that we're on the same page. I'd like to use email to communicate unless it's an emergency (then texting or calling is fine). So, I'll send you an email each Monday morning and I'd appreciate your feedback within a day or so. In addition, I want our communication to focus only on the kids; talking about our relationship or other topics isn't helpful right now. So, I won't discuss anything except the kids or respond to other topics if you bring them up.

Thank you for working with me to meet the needs of our kids.

Mei

When you establish what you want and need in your relationship with your ex, it'll be easier for you to communicate those expectations and follow through when your boundaries are violated. Again, your ex may not change their behavior, but you can always change yours.

Once you've set more transparent boundaries with your ex, you'll benefit tremendously by having supportive people around you. When starting a new life without your ex, it's imperative to find people who'll not only help you get through the tough times but will also bring joy back into your life. Let's find some ways to increase your social support.

Increasing Your Social Support

It's very likely that your breakup has wreaked havoc on your social life. Not only is your ex—who was probably a large source of social interaction for you—gone, but the end of your relationship has shifted your friendships, social schedule, and lifestyle in enormous ways (Field et al. 2011). Relationships with mutual friends who were a regular part of your life before your breakup may have changed dramatically, even irrevocably. You may be avoiding places you used to frequent, and you're probably feeling emotionally vulnerable, which makes the idea of going out to meet new people uncomfortable or even unpleasant. You may not feel like socializing much right now.

Yet, as humans, we're social beings. Feeling close to people who share our interests, experiences, and passions make our lives more fun and fulfilling. In fact, feeling connected to a community or social group is one of the most important predictors of positive mental health outcomes and can be immensely beneficial to your healing process (Harandi, Taghinasab, and Nayeri 2017). Reestablishing relationships with friends, family members, colleagues, neighbors, and other people you were close to before your breakup while making new connections can help you cope. In fact, many organizations and 12-step groups, like Co-Dependents Anonymous (https:// coda.org) and Sex and Love Addicts Anonymous (https://slaafws.org), were created to support people struggling with love addiction. These groups offer social support, and their programs integrate well with CBT, which makes them a welcome supplement to the information you're learning in this book.

In addition to cultivating old relationships and building new ones, connecting with a spiritual belief system or religious community is an important part of the healing process for many people (Miller 1999). The 12-step movement is built on the assertion that there's a God (Alcoholics Anonymous World Services, Inc. 2003). Independent of what specific beliefs you may have about a higher power, most religious and spiritual traditions believe that it's a benevolent, forgiving, loving force that has the best of intentions for you and everyone around you. Although your relationship with spirituality is very personal, acknowledging that you're powerless over your ex and trusting that a power greater than yourself is hovering over you and helping from behind the scenes can be comforting (Miller 1999; Myss 2008). If having a spiritual practice resonates with you or is something you're open to exploring, I encourage you to use it as part of your healing process. In the AA tradition, most meetings open with the "Serenity Prayer": *God, grant me the serenity to accept the things I cannot change, the courage to change the things I can, and the wisdom to know the difference.* Sometimes just saying a prayer asking for guidance and grace can get you through your darkest moments (Myss 2008).

EXERCISE: Getting Social Support

Given that your support system may be shifting dramatically right now, think about who you want in your social support network moving forward. Are there people you can lean on when you're most upset? Are there organizations or groups that you'd like to connect with more? Topics you'd like to explore? In time, having a network may also help you to mentor others going through exaholic breakups; offering encouragement to others can solidify your own growth while making everyone involved feel good (Alcoholics Anonymous World Services, Inc. 2003). Then, in your journal, describe the ways you'd like to get more social interaction and write any support-seeking efforts in your log as self-care interventions.

In addition to a changing support network, it's likely that your physical health has suffered since your breakup. We want to address that next.

Taking Care of Your Physical Health

Your physical health may be the last thing on your mind right now, but your body may have weakened since your breakup (Bobby 2015; Field 2017). You may have stopped exercising regularly or taking care of your basic physical needs, like showering, shaving, or even getting dressed. You may have no appetite, emotionally eat, or binge eat—not eating for a day, eating only when you feel especially good or bad, or devouring an entire gallon of ice cream in an impulsive moment before bed. It's also common to engage in other behaviors that feel addictive because they tend to co-occur (Kim et al. 2020; Zarate et al. 2022). In other words, if you struggle with love addiction you may also struggle with other addictive behaviors, like gambling, smoking, drinking, shopping, sexual promiscuity, or online gaming, all of which can have negative consequences on your health and well-being.

This is a good time to acknowledge how essential your physical health is to your healing journey, because you need to be strong to get through this. Moving forward, seeking out medical attention for any serious health concerns while taking better care of your body is important.

EXERCISE: Getting Healthier

Think about your body and overall health. Have you been getting too little or too much exercise? Sleeping well? Gaining or losing weight? Are you eating fresh fruits and vegetables? Taking vitamins or supplements to ensure that you're getting enough nutrition in your diet? In your journal describe the ways you've been physically healthy and unhealthy since this breakup. Then take action to develop healthier sleep, eating, and exercise habits. Record them in your log as self-care interventions.

In addition to taking good care of your physical health, meeting your mental health needs is a priority. Sometimes during breakups people transition from symptoms typical of experiences of loss to intensely damaging struggles, and they would greatly benefit from professional help (Earp et al. 2017; Kansky and Allen 2018; Marshall 2012). Let's address that next.

Finding a Skilled Therapist

I'll always argue that therapy is a gift you give yourself. *It's the only relationship you'll have in your entire life that exists solely to benefit you!* So, if you're interested in therapy, I encourage you to find a skilled mental health professional. That said, if you're experiencing any of the following serious symptoms, please consider seeking out professional support now:

- You're worried that you could hurt yourself or others and have a plan to do so.

- You're having severe symptoms and are unable to meet your basic needs. For example, you can't get out of bed or have stopped eating.

- You feel profoundly depressed, feel anxious, or are having trauma-based responses to your breakup. For example, you feel jumpy or constantly on alert, struggle to concentrate, or have no hope for your future.

- You've stopped going to or performing adequately at work or school.

- You're drinking or using drugs in an excessive, problematic way.

- You can't care for dependents adequately, including your children, older adults, or pets.

- You're stalking your ex by continuing to pursue contact with them even though they've asked you to stop.

Working with a therapist can be incredibly helpful as you move on from this breakup. I recommend looking for someone with a background in CBT, addictions, and relationships. If you have insurance, find out who it covers and read through their biographies. When you find someone who looks like they'd be a good fit, make an appointment. If your session doesn't go well or feel right, it's okay to try another therapist. In fact, you can have introductory sessions with multiple therapists until you find someone who pushes you in a supportive but active way. If you pursue therapy, record your efforts in your log as a self-care intervention.

Moving Forward

You're now well on your way to effectively managing your symptoms in the present moment. You are more aware of your symptoms, are assessing how they function in your life using your log, and are practicing a host of new skills to actively stop them. You're also adding some positive, self-affirming people and activities back into your life again. Congratulations on your efforts! Your continued hard work will pay off enormously over time.

In part 2 of this book, we're going to take a deeper dive into how you became addicted to your ex and what keeps you stuck on them. That requires carefully examining your thoughts and beliefs about yourself, your ex, and this breakup. To really move on and avoid being here again with your next dating partner, we've got to challenge the untrue and unhelpful contents of your thoughts themselves.

Part 2

Challenging Beliefs That Keep You Stuck

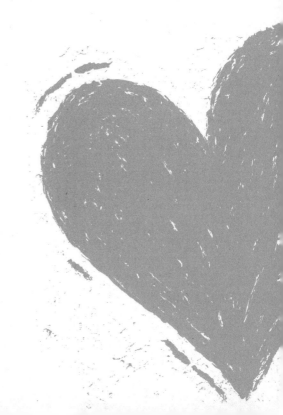

CHAPTER 4

Thinking Clearly About Your Breakup

My ex texted me last night for the first time in three months. I was so relieved to hear from her. For a moment I thought that my prayers had been answered and she wanted to get back together. Sadly, that wasn't the case. So, I practiced setting boundaries. I told her that I love her but can't communicate with her right now and won't respond to her messages in the future. It was hard to do, but I know it's better for me in the long run.

I haven't contacted my ex in forty-nine days. Radically accepting this breakup is such a challenge for me. I keep thinking of ways to seduce and win him back instead of living with the reality that we're not together anymore. So, I'll keep practicing until it gets easier.

I went to my first Co-Dependents Anonymous meeting today. I was nervous about going, but once I was there it was comforting to meet other people struggling like I am. It helped me see that I'm not alone. We're all struggling to let go of the past in some way.

At this point, you're probably more aware of your exaholic symptoms and how they function in your life than ever before. You see how the desire to be close to your ex fuels a miserable barrage of thoughts, cravings, feelings, and behaviors that ultimately leave you feeling terrible. And now that you can see your exaholic cycle in action, you're actively practicing many skills to stop it. Like the exaholics in the stories above, you're setting clearer boundaries, getting more social support, radically trying to accept this breakup, and responding differently to triggers. All of this probably feels strange because it's so new and different, but you're doing it anyway because you're committed to moving on without your ex so you can have a more fulfilling present and future.

You may have also realized that letting go of your ex requires a lot of time and active effort. Maybe more than you were bargaining for before starting this book! Tracking your experiences every day with a self-monitoring log is an intense and sometimes unpleasant task, not to mention that you're responding to your symptoms in a completely new way. It's a lot of work! Believe me, I get it. And I don't want you to stop! The more you practice, the easier it gets, because you become stronger. More grounded. Better able to respond to life situations in helpful and self-appreciating ways. As a result, you'll have more time and energy to enjoy the wonderful things that already exist in your life while creating a brighter future. Really, that's the ultimate goal of this work, and you're doing it.

So far we've focused on understanding your addictive symptoms in the present moment and on helping you feel better. Now, in part 2 of this book, we're going to explore how you got here in the first place. We'll start by unraveling the contents of your thoughts about this breakup, because although we all want to believe we're right about everything—that our perceptions and opinions are factually based and valid—our thinking is often highly flawed and inaccurate. So, the next step on your healing journey is to become aware of, assess, and challenge flawed thinking patterns that keep you stuck on your ex. Let's start now.

It's All About Perspective

It's easy to think that the loss of your ex is "causing" your miserable exaholic symptoms. And in some ways, that's true; if you were still dating your ex, you probably wouldn't feel so bad right now. But in other ways it's false, because it's not the end of your relationship itself that's causing your symptoms; it's the way *you think about your breakup* that enflames or extinguishes heartache.

That may sound more like a word exercise than something meaningful, so let's unpack it. From a CBT perspective, your breakup is a situation that occurred in your life. I know—it's a major life event that's shifted everything about your daily experiences in profound ways, but it's a situation nonetheless. And, like all events that happen in life, the situation exists outside of your mind. It has no inherent value, no meaning or weight in and of itself. It's merely an event *until you react to it.* How you think about this breakup will largely determine how you react to it. In this way, the thoughts that immediately run through your mind when you think about your ex— the *automatic thoughts* you've been recording in your logs—are largely responsible for how good or bad you feel and how you want to act (A. T. Beck 1976; A. T. Beck et al. 1979; J. S. Beck 2021).

Let's consider an example to really see how this applies to your life. Imagine that a friend of yours ran into your ex last week at a local restaurant and thought it looked like they were on a date with someone. Upon hearing the news, you feel a jolt of panic laced with a stabbing pain in your chest. You immediately become aware of your strong symptoms and pause. As soon as you can, you get your self-monitoring log and record the situation like this: "My friend ran into my ex on a date with someone else." Remember that the situation is just a factual description of something that's happening in the world that feels like it's causing a reaction inside you.

After identifying the situation, you write down your automatic thoughts—the thoughts that immediately race through your mind when you think about the situation. These thoughts are what give meaning to your experience in ways that can be helpful or harmful to you (A. T. Beck et al. 1979; J. S. Beck 2021). In response to hearing that your ex is on a date, for example, you might think *My ex has already moved on without me. They're never coming back. My life is over.* If you think that way, how do you think you'll feel and want to act? Well, if you're like most people, you'll feel profoundly depressed and want to head to the nearest bar or stay in bed all day.

Your distress level will be high—around a 9 or 10 on our scale. Your final log might look something like this:

> October 6. Wednesday. 11:00 a.m.   Day 32 no contact.
>
> *Situation:* My friend ran into my ex on a date with someone else.
>
> *Automatic thoughts:* My ex has already moved on without me. They're never coming back. My life is over.
>
> *Symptoms:* I feel hopeless and depressed. I want to drown my sorrows at the nearest bar or hide in my bed.
>
> *Level of distress:* 9–10.
>
> *Self-care intervention:* I'm calling a friend to keep from isolating myself in bed. Hearing that my ex is dating someone new is very triggering to me, so I'm going to get some social support.
>
> *Effect on symptoms:* Seeing my friend gave me some perspective on the situation, which I really needed.

Now, I want you to take the exact same situation and consider what happens to your symptoms if you change your thinking. What if your automatic thoughts were *It's hard for me to hear that my ex is dating already. But we're broken up—they can do whatever they want. Even though it stings, I need to focus on healing myself now and moving on without them.* In this case, you'd probably still feel some sadness and wouldn't like the idea of your ex dating someone new, but you're probably not as upset. Instead of crawling under the covers in a dark room, it's easier for you to acknowledge your feelings and move forward with your day. So, instead of experiencing strong symptoms, your distress stays low—at maybe a 4 or 5—before you've even done a self-care intervention! Your log might look something like this:

> October 6. Wednesday. 11:00 a.m.   Day 32 no contact.
>
> *Situation:* My friend ran into my ex on a date.
>
> *Automatic thoughts:* It's hard for me to hear that my ex is dating already. But we're broken up—they can do whatever they want. Even though it stings, I need to focus on healing myself now and moving on without them.

Symptoms: I feel sad and miss them.

Level of distress: 4-5.

Self-care intervention: I'm practicing thought—stopping and going to do some extra self—care tonight to help me feel good about who I am and the steps I'm taking to move on from this breakup.

Effect on symptoms: The more I use my skills, the stronger I feel.

What I really want you to notice here is that *nothing changed about the situation.* Both scenarios are exactly the same: your friend saw your ex on a date. The only thing that changed is the way you're thinking about it! When you change your perspective to be more helpful and empowering, your emotional reactions, cravings, and urges to act out are also going to shift in healthy ways. This seemingly simple yet massively important change in perspective can have enormous effects on your well-being (Tolin 2016; J. S. Beck 2021).

The great news is that as you become aware of your automatic thoughts, you can assess them for accuracy and challenge them if they're faulty. As you do, your symptoms will naturally weaken—your emotions won't be as negative or reactive, your desire to act in impulsive and compulsive ways will lessen, your cravings won't be as strong, and your body won't be so tense, lethargic, and on edge. So, let's learn to identify and challenge your faulty thinking.

Identifying Red-Flag Exaholic Thinking

One of the core assumptions of CBT is that inaccurate thinking drives our mental health struggles (Ellis and Harper 1997; Tolin 2016). As humans, we want to think that our thoughts are true—that they accurately reflect reality. Unfortunately, many inaccurate thoughts automatically pop into our minds every day without any conscious effort or awareness on our part. This is especially true when we're struggling with intense emotional pain, because our thinking about ourselves, others, and the world around us at those times tends to be unrealistically negative (A. T. Beck 1976; A. T. Beck et al. 1979).

All of us think in flawed ways sometimes. Dr. Aaron Beck (1976) described some of the characteristic ways we think inaccurately, which he referred to as *cognitive distortions*, or what I'm going to call *red-flag thinking*. As you read through the examples below, really consider which kinds of deceptive thinking apply to you the most. When an example resonates with you, make a note in your journal because we're going to practice challenging faulty thinking soon.

Denial. First described in depth by Anna Freud (1937) following the work of her father Sigmund in the late nineteenth century (1894; 2013), refusing to believe the truth is one of the most common ways we distort reality. For example, you may struggle to admit that your relationship is over by thinking things like *We'll get back together. They'll come back.* You may also see your ex as the person you want them to be instead of who they actually are by thinking things like *My ex is the best. I love everything about them.* When you deny the truth, you ignore or blatantly refuse to see reality as it objectively exists outside of yourself. Yet the truth is that no amount of denial will change reality.

Rationalization. Anytime you create a reason or explanation to excuse someone's unacceptable behavior—including your own—you're using rationalization (A. Freud 1937). For example, if your ex cheated on you, you may find yourself defending them by thinking things like *My ex wouldn't have cheated if that girl hadn't thrown herself at him.* You may also try to explain away your own harmful behaviors with justifications like *It's okay that I drank a bottle of wine last night because I had a really bad day and it helped me calm down.* Or *I emailed my ex last night because they need to know how I feel*—even though you know you're better off not communicating with them. The truth is that although we use rationalization to feel better, no explanation will make unacceptable behavior okay.

Emotional reasoning. When you engage in this type of flawed thinking, you conclude that your feelings in the present moment accurately reflect your current life situation (A. T. Beck 1976; A. T. Beck et al. 1979). It's the idea that because something feels true it is true—that strong emotions are reasonable, logical, and being caused by something in your life today. For example, when you're so sad that you can barely get out of bed, you may think *I'm lonely, so I'm always going to be alone. I'll never find love again.* Or after your last fight with your ex you may have thought *I'm so angry! They've ruined my life!* Emotional reasoning blinds you to the idea that your emotions may be triggered by something from your past or be warped in irrational ways. The truth is that when emotional reactions are extreme, they're more likely to be related to unresolved issues from the past and inaccurate interpretations of the present than to the actual situation at hand.

All-or-nothing thinking. The irrational thoughts of this red-flag thinking are extreme and don't consider the nuances of life. When you catch yourself saying the words "always," "never," "all," "none," "right," and "wrong," you're probably engaging in this kind of flawed thinking (A. T. Beck 1976). After a breakup, it's common to focus on the things you loved about your ex. You may think things like *My ex is perfect. If we could just get back together everything would be okay.* Conversely, you may only remember the bad parts of the breakup and think things like *I hate my ex. They're such a jerk and need to pay for how they treated me!* The truth is that life is complicated. It's rare for anything or anyone to be all good or bad, black or white, right or wrong. Generally, the world is full of gray—and so is your ex, so was your relationship, and so are you.

Jumping to conclusions. When you assume that you know the future (*fortune-telling*) or can read someone else's mind (*mind reading*) without adequate evidence, you're using flawed thinking to come up with conclusions that may be wrong (A. T. Beck 1976). It's common to think that your romantic future is bleak after a bad breakup. You may think things like *I'll never find anyone as wonderful as my ex,* or *My ex clearly never loved me.* The truth is that no one knows the future and you can't fully understand another person's experience. Furthermore, your life is only bleak if you see it that way and make choices that harm you.

Personalization. When you think that someone else's behavior is a direct reflection of you in some way without ample evidence, you're using personalization (A. T. Beck 1976). For example, many exaholics think *My ex isn't calling me, so clearly they don't care how I'm doing.* It may be hard to see that there are many reasons your ex may not be calling you or trying to get back together that have little to do with whether they care about you, like they're busy, they don't think you should be together anymore, they've fallen for someone else, or they're also trying to move on!

This kind of inaccurate thinking is particularly tricky for people going through a breakup because, in some ways, your ex's choices probably do reflect how much they want to be with you. For example, you may think *My ex didn't love me enough to make it work.* That may be true to some degree, but your ex's feelings don't define your lovability or desirability as a person. The truth is that many of us struggle to believe that we have fundamental value after a breakup, especially if we were left or didn't want our relationship to end (Perilloux and Buss 2008). That's why rebuilding your self-esteem and sense of self-efficacy is essential to moving forward—something you're already doing by using the skills in this book.

Magnification and minimization. You're engaging in these types of flawed thinking when you evaluate yourself or others in an extreme way that exaggerates the negative or discounts the positive, respectively (A. T. Beck 1976). For example, after contacting your ex in a moment of weakness, you may magnify or see the worst possible outcomes by thinking something like *I completely ruined my progress toward getting over them.* Or, as you reflect on your symptoms, you may think *This breakup is the worst thing that could ever happen to me.* Conversely, you may find yourself minimizing your efforts to get over your ex, saying things like *I don't even know why I bother doing my self-monitoring log because I keep looking at my ex's social media posts.* So, I'm *failing at this, too.* The truth is, you deserve credit for every effort you make to get over your ex. Occasional slipups don't erase the positive changes you've been making. Your intention matters. Your effort matters. And, as you start feeling better, you have yourself to thank for it.

Labeling. This flawed thinking results in you giving someone a fixed global title that defines them (A. T. Beck 1976). Often it's negative and looks like name-calling. For example, you may call yourself a *loser*, an *addict*, a *fool*, or *pathetic*—and you may call your ex the same things! But the truth is, we're far too complex for our entire personality and identity to be condensed into one oversimplified label.

Specialness fallacy. This type of thinking involves thinking that you're an exception to the rules and goings-on of human life (Yalom 1980). You're most likely to think this way if you believe that bad things can't happen to you because you're somehow special and protected from harm. Following a breakup you didn't see coming, you may think *How could my ex leave me! This can't be happening to me!* The truth is that almost anything can happen to any of us at any time, including falling in love and breaking up.

Accepting norms. When you internalize or personally accept the norms and values of your culture as facts instead of critically thinking about whether you believe them to be true or not, you're accepting norms (Sue and Sue 2012). We're all raised in familial, social, and cultural environments that hold specific values. If you grew up in a religious household that values marriage, for example, going through a breakup or divorce may lead you to think things like *I've failed. Divorce is bad and I deserve to be miserable.* Or if you're a single person in your forties, you may think *Something's wrong with me because I'm not married.* The truth is that, although the values of your culture affect how you're treated and viewed socially, you ultimately decide what matters to you in this life—and it may be in direct conflict with what society tells you to believe.

These are just a smattering of the many ways your automatic thoughts can be flawed and make your symptoms worse. Let's turn our attention to exploring your red-flag exaholic thinking.

EXERCISE: Identifying Your Red-Flag Thoughts

You've been recording your automatic thoughts in your self-monitoring log for some time now. Look through your completed logs and compare your entries to the types of flawed thinking we just explored. Then, using examples of your exaholic thinking, create a "red-flag thought list." Record the exact wording of your thoughts and note any observations you have about them. Look for and record any categories of flawed thinking that you tend to use often. For example, are you in denial? Do you often rationalize unhealthy behavior? Do you label yourself or others? Do you minimize your efforts to heal and magnify the importance of your ex in your life?

Now that you've identified some of your red-flag thoughts, it's time to learn how to evaluate their accuracy and to challenge them.

Assessing Your Thoughts for Accuracy

Ultimately, you want to respond to situations in life with objectively accurate perceptions that don't throw you into the exaholic cycle. Like a good detective solving a mystery, you'll do this by testing the accuracy of your thinking, looking for data that support or negate each thought. Anytime you have evidence that your thought is false, misleading, or flawed, you're going to challenge it (J. S. Beck 2021). I'm not suggesting that you're supposed to think positively all the time—breaking up is still an incredibly difficult experience—but that you want your thoughts to reflect your situation in an accurate, self-empowering way (Ellis and Harper 1997).

To begin assessing your thoughts, you're going to ask yourself two fundamental questions. First: *Is my thinking accurate?* You're going to answer this by looking for evidence indicating your thought is true or false. Second: *Is my thinking helpful?* You're going to answer this question by determining whether your thinking makes your symptoms better or worse. To help you get the hang of this, let's practice using Liam's story as an example.

Liam is a handsome fifty-two-year-old with stylish wire-rimmed glasses. He met Jose in the brightly lit conference room of a massive Las Vegas hotel. As Jose took the stage to speak, his poise in front of the massive crowd charmed Liam. That afternoon during a coffee break, Liam locked eyes with Jose and a discrete flirtation began. The two met later that night in Jose's room, leading to a clandestine romance that lasted more than three years.

Jose was a bit of a player who didn't want anything to do with commitment. The challenge of getting Jose to be exclusive made the relationship exciting and seductive to Liam, but also heartbreaking. Liam became more uncomfortable over time because he knew Jose had other lovers, but the idea of separating from him was equally unbearable. Toward the end, Liam told Jose he didn't want to date anymore unless they were committed and openly together. When Liam set his relationship boundary, Jose broke it off. Although Liam intellectually believed it was the right choice for them to split, he felt completely addicted to Jose.

To overcome his love addiction, Liam examined his automatic thoughts for their accuracy and to see how they affected his symptoms. Let's look at one of his logs:

September 21. Sunday. 11:00 a.m.   Day 45 no contact.

Situation: I'm giving a presentation in less than a week and need to prepare.

Automatic thoughts: I can't stop thinking about Jose; this presentation is a trigger. I miss him so much. I can't live without him.

Symptoms: I'm feeling profoundly sad. I want to call him and hear his voice.

Level of distress: 8.

> *Self-care intervention:* I'm choosing to ride out the craving and practicing radically accepting that it's over.
>
> *Effect on symptoms:* My distress went down to a 6. I know that I can get through this.

Looking at Liam's automatic thoughts, we'll start by asking our two questions: Is this thinking accurate? Is this thinking helpful? Liam's first two thoughts (*I can't stop thinking about Jose; this presentation is a trigger. I miss him so much.*) seem to reflect his feelings and desires in an honest way, and his awareness that giving this presentation is a trigger is excellent. But these thoughts aren't helpful because they lead Liam to think about and crave Jose more, making his symptoms worse. The last thought (*I can't live without him.*) gets a red flag; Liam is jumping to conclusions about his future and magnifying Jose's importance to his survival! Plus, neither thought is helpful. So, his thinking needs to shift.

Let's look at another of Liam's entries. Again, we're assessing Liam's thinking by asking if it's accurate and helpful.

> September 26. Friday. 10:00 p.m.   Day 50 no contact.
>
> *Situation:* I'm home alone preparing for tomorrow.
>
> *Automatic thoughts:* Maybe being one of many is okay. Maybe I'd be happier being his side hookup than nothing. I'm never going to get over him. I'm going to be single forever.
>
> *Symptoms:* I'm confused and panicky. And angry that he didn't want me as his husband.
>
> *Level of distress:* 9.
>
> *Self-care intervention:* I'm going to take a shower, use my rumination time to vent about this situation, and then practice thought-stopping, because I need to focus on preparing for my presentation tomorrow.
>
> *Effect on symptoms:* My distress is down to a 5. I'm able to focus on work again.

It's unclear whether Liam's first automatic thought is true for him or not (*Maybe being one of many is okay. Maybe I'd be happier being his side hookup than nothing.*). But being in love with someone who doesn't want to be exclusively committed when that's what you want doesn't tend to feel good, so it's not helpful. His final two thoughts (*I'm never going to get over him. I'm going to be single forever.*) both get red flags; they reflect emotional reasoning and fortune-telling, and they're definitely not helpful.

EXERCISE: The Costs of Your Flawed Thinking

Take out your journal and review the red-flag thought list you created. To examine the costs of your flawed thinking, ask yourself our two assessment questions: Is this thinking accurate? Is this thinking helpful? You already know that your red-flag thoughts aren't accurate, so hopefully you can see that all of them get a no in response to the first question! As you consider the second question, look at how each thought affects your symptoms. Does thinking this way make you want to contact your ex? Crave your ex more? Feel more depressed, anxious, sad, angry, or dejected? Want to act in harmful ways? Identify how each red-flag thought affects you and describe your observations. Record this exercise as a self-care intervention in your log.

Thinking More Clearly

Now that you've identified some of your red-flag thoughts and see how they make your symptoms worse, it's time to challenge them. In CBT terms, we call this *cognitive restructuring*: the process of shifting your thinking to be as accurate and helpful as possible (A. T. Beck 1976; A. T. Beck et al. 1979). To do this, you're going to use the "3 Ds"—*detect, debate,* and *discriminate*—originally developed by Dr. Albert Ellis (Ellis and Harper 1997). You've already *detected,* or identified, your red-flag thinking. Now you're going to *debate* the accuracy of each thought by looking for evidence whether it's true or false, then *discriminate* the true from the untrue by rewriting your thought in the most accurate, self-appreciating way possible. Once you've done this, you'll look at the effect that modifying your thinking has on your symptoms. Hopefully you'll see that you are less emotionally reactive, have fewer cravings, and are less likely to act in harmful ways.

This takes some practice, so let's use Liam's thoughts as an example. Looking at his completed logs, he detected three red-flag thoughts that were highly inaccurate and unhelpful: *I can't live without him, I'm never going to get over him,* and *I'm going to be single forever.* Using the 3 Ds, Liam challenged his first red-flag thought like this:

> **Detect thought:**
> I can't live without him.
>
> **Debate thought:**
> *Evidence that this thought is true:*
> I've struggled with exaholic symptoms since we broke up, so I'm struggling to live without Jose.
>
> *Evidence that this thought is false:*
> I've lived without Jose for the last fifty days and I'm still alive, so I can live without him.
>
> I had a full life before I met Jose, so I've lived without him before.
>
> I may not want to live without him, but I'm capable of doing it.
>
> No matter who I'm dating, I always have myself. I'm really the only person I can't live without.
>
> **Discriminate (by creating a more accurate and helpful thought based on the evidence you've gathered):**
> I loved Jose deeply. I miss him and I've struggled since our breakup. But I lived without him in the past and I can live without him now. Ultimately, I'm responsible for creating a meaningful life for myself with or without him, and I'm actively working to do that.

As you can see, once Liam really looked for evidence that his thought was true, he found there wasn't much data to support its accuracy. Quite the contrary; there was a lot of evidence showing that his thinking was false! Once he saw the data, Liam created a more accurate and helpful perspective that challenged this red-flag thought. As he practiced modifying his thinking, his symptoms weakened and Liam felt more grounded and self-confident over time.

Let's practice the 3 Ds again using Liam's second thought:

Detect:
I'm never going to get over him.

Debate:
Evidence that this thought is true:
I'm not over him now.

Evidence that this thought is false:
I can get over him if I practice the skills I'm learning.

I've gone through breakups before and have found ways to move on.

It's likely that I'll feel better over time if I focus on myself and strive to create a life without him.

Discriminate:
I'm not over Jose today. But research suggests that I can get over him if I use CBT skills to stop my symptoms. So, I can get over him in time if I practice these skills.

Looking at the evidence, Liam found that with this thought he was projecting a future outcome as if it was a fact, and Liam didn't find any evidence that it was true. As he challenged this red-flag thought, he felt better about himself and felt more hopeful about his future.

Let's consider Liam's last thought:

Detect:
I'm going to be single forever.

Debate:
Evidence that this thought is true:

I'm single now.

Evidence that this thought is false:

I dated many people before Jose and I can date again when I'm ready.

I don't have to be single forever. Being in a relationship is a choice.

I met Jose and was attracted to him, so it's likely that I can meet another person I find attractive in the future.

Discriminate:

I'm single now, but I've dated many people who I liked. I can choose to date and try to find another partner when I'm ready. I don't have to be single forever.

After using the 3 Ds to create more accurate and helpful thoughts, Liam's symptoms were much less intense. He still felt sad and wished he were with Jose, but his perspective started to shift in honest, self-empowering ways.

EXERCISE: Challenging Red-Flag Thinking

As we did for Liam, use the 3 Ds to assess and challenge your red-flag thoughts. You can do this in your journal or download the Challenging Your Exaholic Thinking Worksheet that I use, available at this book's website: http://www.newharbinger.com/50379.

For each red-flag thought you've identified, go through the following steps to make them more accurate and helpful:

- **Detect:** Identify an automatic red-flag thought you want to shift.

- **Debate:** Consider evidence that supports your thought (signs that it's true) and evidence that refutes it (signs that it's false or distorted in some way) to determine if it's accurate. (Odds are you'll find more evidence that it's false than true!)

- **Discriminate:** After teasing apart the true from the untrue, rewrite your thought in an honest, self-affirming way.

After you've practiced, look at the effect that changing your thinking has on your symptoms. Do you feel better? Crave your ex less strongly? Feel more grounded and less reactive? Write down any shifts in your symptoms and experience that happen immediately and over time. Practice the 3 Ds as soon as you become aware that you're thinking in untrue or unhelpful ways. Note your efforts in your log as a self-care intervention.

Moving Forward

Learning to assess and change your thinking is critical to stopping the exaholic cycle and to reducing your symptoms. Shifting your automatic thoughts will naturally lead to a more accurate and self-valuing worldview over time. Remember that cheerleading yourself through your breakup by trying to just be positive and get over it is not the goal of challenging your red-flag thinking; you're going through a difficult experience, and it's healthy to acknowledge that. Instead, the goal is to make your thinking as accurate and helpful as possible so that any negative emotions you experience emerge as authentic reactions to truthful reflections about your breakup. What you don't want is to waste your energy feeling terrible because of thoughts that aren't even true!

In the next chapter, we're going to chip away at some of your more stubborn red-flag thoughts. Sometimes you can rationally see that your thinking isn't true or helpful, yet it somehow still *feels true*. To change those more tenacious red-flag thoughts, we need to dig deeper to uncover some of your fundamental beliefs about your ex that drive your faulty thinking.

CHAPTER 5

Seeing Your Ex as They Really Are

It's been a year since I saw my ex. One of my most memorable rock-bottom moments came on a rainy Saturday night when my ex-girlfriend stopped by. We were trying to be friends, which was a disaster because we weren't friends—we were former lovers trying to "act like" friends. And, at the time, I thought I could get her back. When I tried, she made it clear that it was over and left. I started to panic. My mind raced as I gulped air trying to breathe. I wanted to chase after her. Looking back my thinking was really flawed. The truth was I couldn't get her back because she didn't want me anymore. Admitting that really hurt, but I needed to see the truth before I could move on.

I thought I'd never find love until I met my ex. I was late picking my daughter up from school and there he was, playing soccer outside with his kids on the grassy field. I remember thinking that I wanted a partner just like him. We dated for a few years, and after we broke up I still believed he was the only man for me. Until one day when I realized that he's a different person in my mind than he is in real life.

It's been almost seven months since I talked to my ex. Last night I went on my first date since our breakup. Sitting across from each other at a corner table in a cute new restaurant, it probably looked like the perfect evening. He was cute and friendly. In fact, he was great! But all I could think was that he isn't my ex and no one will ever compare.

At some point in your relationship with your ex, you may have thought they were perfect for you. Like the exaholics in the stories above, you may have believed that you'd found your soulmate, your life partner, or your best friend. That you'd always be together. That your relationship was destined to work because you loved each other so much. Unfortunately, as you're probably seeing very clearly now, our thoughts are often highly flawed and inaccurate. Using data you're collecting from your self-monitoring logs, you're becoming increasingly aware of your faulty red-flag thinking and adept at evaluating it using the 3 Ds—detecting the thoughts, debating their accuracy, and discriminating the true from the untrue to form a more honest perspective of your breakup over time.

As you practice making your thoughts more accurate and helpful, you may notice that some of your thinking is relatively easy to change: you spot a red-flag thought and can modify it quickly after looking at the evidence. And hopefully you're also noticing that you feel better after you do so because it changes your exaholic cycle—your symptoms shift as your perspective changes! But you may also notice that some of your red-flag thoughts seem particularly stubborn. When you look at the evidence, they still seem true even though you rationally know they aren't. For example, if you notice yourself thinking something like *I can't live without my ex*, you probably rationally know that it isn't true. You lived without your ex in the past, you're living without them now, and you can live without them in the future! But it may still feel true, and that feeling can make it extremely hard to move on.

These tenacious red-flag thoughts are usually harder to change because they're born from some deeper, more fundamental beliefs you hold about your ex and romantic relationships. Underneath your automatic thoughts are some inflexible conclusions you've made about yourself and other people referred to as *schemas*, or *core beliefs* (A. T. Beck et al. 1979; J. S. Beck 2021; Young, Klosko, and Weishaar 2003). These beliefs exist outside of your conscious awareness, but they're incredibly powerful because they affect how you perceive your life. Think of your thoughts like an iceberg: your core beliefs are the bigger, underlying ice mass beneath the water that supports your visible, icy red-flag thoughts. To change your most stubborn red-flag thinking, you've got to uncover what you believe about your ex and your breakup itself that's supporting the thoughts in your mind (A. T. Beck et al. 1979; Tolin 2016). So, we're diving into your core beliefs next.

Faulty Beliefs About Your Ex

You're now fully aware that falling in love is one of the most intoxicating natural experiences you may ever have in life—an emotional, sexual, and physical connection to one special person who consumes your energy (Fisher 2004). Usually you feel the most enamored in the first few months of dating, during the "honeymoon phase" (Fisher 2016). This is partly because you're fully immersed in a new experience that's stimulating your mind, body, and brain in ways that feel wonderful! But it's also because you're most prone to adopting faulty, idealized beliefs about your lover during this time that make you want them more.

What do I mean by that? Well, early in romantic relationships, you don't really know your lover yet. You know some selective information about them that they've chosen to share, and you've drawn some conclusions about them by observing how they act, eat, speak, or even dress. But the truth is that early in a relationship you generally know very little about the person you're dating. When it's someone you like or are attracted to, you tend to fill in the blanks with *who you want them to be*—as if they have the characteristics of your ideal mate—instead of seeing them as they really are. That's why most of what you believe when you're in love is overly positive, highly idealistic, and quite inaccurate!

You've probably drawn many faulty conclusions about your ex that drive your more obstinate red-flag thinking and keep you stuck in the exaholic cycle. As you read about some of the faulty beliefs that I observe most frequently in people struggling with love addiction, see which resonate with your experience. Keep in mind that these aren't beliefs you necessarily want to think are true, but they often are operating under the surface making your red-flag thoughts *feel true* even when they aren't!

Faulty belief 1: My ex is the best. When you fell in love, you probably thought your ex was wonderful. Maybe even the best person you'd ever met. Part of the magical experience of falling in love is thinking someone's exceptional. It's hard to imagine falling for a person you think is mediocre or below average! As a result, you probably put your ex on a pedestal and saw them as special, highly important, and better than other dating partners (Mellody, Miller, and Miller 2003). In doing so, you overvalued your ex's general importance in the world because you found them so captivating, intriguing, and compelling. Even the annoying things they did when you were together weren't that bad because you saw your ex in such a positive light. Believing they're the best not only made you love them more, but it also made you feel better about yourself because you were connected to this person you deemed incredible. This core belief drives stubborn red-flag thoughts like *No one's as good as my ex*, and *No one else will ever compare or make me feel the way she did.*

The truth is, your ex is just a person, full of faults like the rest of us. They may be special and unique in wonderful ways, but valuing them above all other humans—including yourself—leads to you feeling fundamentally less desirable after your breakup because you're no longer attached to this idealized person. In addition, having an overly positive perception of your ex gives them too much power in your life and makes you want their approval. When you start to date again, for example, new potential mates have no chance of impressing you because you've already concluded that no one is as good as your ex! Continuing to think that they're the best doesn't serve you well; it isn't true and it isn't helpful.

Faulty belief 2: My ex is perfect—and perfect for me. At some point in your relationship you probably believed your ex was the perfect partner for you—and maybe even the perfect person! Early in romantic relationships, we tend to create a fantasy version of our lover in our mind. It may be that you saw your ex as your rescuer, an esteemed professional, an intellectual, a role model, or even a fellow pet lover. Some of what you saw and believed about them was true; your ex may really be that exercise guru or romantic traveler you've always wanted. But whatever you saw, it probably fit your model of the perfect person instead of accurately capturing your ex as they actually exist in the world. This core belief fuels dogged red-flag thoughts like *My ex is my one and only true love,* and *When he acts like a jerk, it's not really him—he's really wonderful on the inside.*

The truth is that your ex isn't perfect—no one is. And given that you're broken up, your ex isn't perfect for you either, at least not today. Looking back at your relationship, you may focus on the parts of your ex you loved while selectively forgetting the many things about them that weren't ideal for you. When you did see a flaw, you probably overlooked it or even found it charming. That annoying habit of cracking their knuckles, swallowing loudly, leaving the kitchen sink a mess after making a sandwich, or using your car and never filling up the gas tank is somehow cute when your ex does it but beyond annoying coming from anyone else. You may have even made excuses for them when they treated you poorly to keep the image of perfection intact in your mind (Mellody, Miller, and Miller 2003). If you can't remember why you broke up or anything negative about your ex when you think back on your relationship, you're probably holding on to this faulty belief.

Faulty belief 3: My ex's choices reflect my value. When you're in love, it's common to develop a *couple's identity* with your partner to reflect that you're a team (Levine and Heller 2012). This process can be healthy when you're in a relationship and building a life with someone. You shift your lifestyle to reflect who you are, who your partner is, and what works for you as a couple. The problem is that you may have mistakenly started to see your lover's feelings, thoughts, and behaviors as a reflection of you and your value. You may be hypersensitive and reactive to your ex's choices, opinions, and behaviors because everything they do feels like a personal attack even when it often has nothing to do with you. If your ex doesn't want to be with you anymore, you may find yourself personalizing that decision or changing to make them want you again, even if it means not being true to yourself. For example, to win their affection you may stop being friends with people your ex doesn't like, change the way you dress or act in social situations, or do things sexually that aren't comfortable for you. This core belief fuels stubborn red-flag thoughts like *I'm nothing without my ex*, and *If my ex doesn't love me, I'm unlovable.*

It's hard not to fall into this trap sometimes, especially during a love-addicted breakup. Culturally, the notion that when two people fall in love they become one is socially reinforced, fueling the faulty belief that you're not whole without a partner (Fisher 2004; Fisher 2016). Yet the truth is that the way your ex acts, feels, and thinks is fundamentally a reflection of who they are—*not of who you are*. Your ex is separate from you with their own identity, feelings, thoughts, and experiences. What's more, whether your ex loves you, likes you, thinks you're amazing, or wants nothing to do with you, *your value's the same. You* determine your value—it's not dependent on your ex and never has been.

Faulty belief 4: My ex will change—or I can change them! If you really didn't like something about your ex and you knew it, it's very likely you had a fundamental belief that they would change. Or, better yet, that you could change them! Even now you may believe that you can make them change—love you again, want you more, stop drinking, be more affectionate, tell you all the things they love about you, be more romantic, or be more emotionally available. This belief also leads you to incorrectly think that getting back together would be universally positive! Stubborn red-flag thoughts that emerge from this belief include *My ex will come back to me*, *I can make them want me again*, and *They just need time to come around; they'll change.*

The truth is that you can't make anyone change. People change when they actively want to, choose to, and are willing to do the daily work required to make it happen (Norcross, Krebs, and Prochaska 2011). It's possible that your ex will change. It's even possible that you'll get back together someday and form a healthy bond. But if these things happen, it'll be because your ex chose to change, you chose to change, and the two of you intentionally worked to have a more functional relationship—not because you changed your ex.

Faulty belief 5: Fighting with my ex means they love me. Many exaholics are more comfortable with chaotic highs and lows than stable relationship connections (Bobby 2015; Fisher et al. 2016). It's part of the nature of addiction; your brain responds to new stimuli in more excited ways than it does to older, more predictable stimuli. In other words, your body's more stimulated when you're on edge, doing something new, or in a less secure relationship (Fisher 2016). So as much as you consciously don't like fighting or conflict, the more unstable, unpredictable, and chaotic your relationship is with your ex, the more likely you are to stay stuck on them.

The truth is that dramatic interactions with your ex aren't reflective of safe, bonded love. Persistent red-flag thoughts driven from this belief include *If we didn't love each other so much we wouldn't fight like this*, and *My ex only acts that way because she loves me so much.* Anytime you're experiencing drama with your ex—fighting, conflict, and certainly abuse—and conclude that it's because you love one another deeply, you're probably ensnared by this core belief.

Faulty belief 6: I need my ex to be complete. After falling in love and breaking up, you're likely to feel lost for a while. Everything in your life may feel bland and lack meaning, leading you to believe that you need your ex to be happy and feel complete (Bobby 2015). This faulty belief fuels red-flag thoughts like *If I were still with my ex everything would be okay*, and *I need my ex to be happy.*

The truth is that you don't need your ex to live a fulfilling life. In fact, you're going to struggle to be in a healthy relationship with anyone if you aren't grounded and secure in your relationship with yourself. You also set yourself up for failure with this belief by making your well-being and value dependent on someone else. Anytime you look outside yourself to feel whole and healed you lose your power. Any red-flag thoughts that suggest you need your ex to be complete and fulfilled are being fueled by this faulty belief.

Faulty belief 7: My relationship would work if my ex loved me enough. Most of us want to believe that love is enough to make a relationship work. We want to think that love conquers all. That being passionate about someone creates the foundation of a relationship that's bound to be successful. That if your ex loved you enough, they'd never leave. They'd be inspired to be their best self. They'd find a way to get back together because they can't live without you. This faulty belief fuels red-flag thoughts like *If my ex loved me enough they wouldn't leave*, and *As long as we love each other we can make it work*.

The truth is that love alone isn't enough to build a healthy relationship. For many of us, love is a necessary condition for being in a romantic relationship—you want to feel passionate about the people you date—but it's far from being sufficient to sustain a healthy relationship. And love isn't always necessary: many arranged marriages are based on people having similar values rather than love-based connections, and many of these couples have fulfilling, successful romantic relationships (Regan, Lakhanpal, and Anguiano 2012)! So, when your red-flag thoughts suggest that your relationship would work if your ex loved you more, you're tapping into this faulty belief.

Do you relate to some of these faulty beliefs about your ex? Do you see your ex as the ideal? Do you think they're the one and only perfect mate for you? Do you think their opinion of you somehow reflects your actual value? Do you believe they'll change? Let's identify some of your specific faulty beliefs now.

EXERCISE: Faulty Beliefs About Your Ex

Looking at the examples above, describe in your journal some of the faulty beliefs you have about your ex. Try to elaborate on them by recounting events, observations, or examples that highlight these flawed conclusions and how they affect you. Take your time to really dive into your beliefs. You may not consciously believe they're true because they're operating under the surface (Remember the iceberg metaphor?), but they're driving your most tenacious red-flag thoughts, so you need to become aware of them so you can change them. Record this exercise in your log as a self-care intervention.

Now that you're becoming more aware of your faulty beliefs about your ex, we're going to link them more directly to your red-flag thinking. This can be tricky, so we're going to practice together.

Connecting Red-Flag Thoughts to Faulty Beliefs

Becoming aware of and changing faulty beliefs about your ex is much harder than shifting red-flag automatic thoughts for two key reasons. First, your core beliefs aren't usually obvious to you because they're so foundational (A. T. Beck 1976; J. S. Beck 2021). They're underwater! So, they're unlikely to show up directly on your self-monitoring log; you have to search for them by looking through your most stubborn red-flag thoughts and identify what's driving them. Second, unlike automatic thoughts, which you can evaluate using your reactions to current life situations, your core beliefs have been developing over the course of your entire life (J. S. Beck 2021). So, changing faulty beliefs about your ex has a lot to do with shifting your deepest early childhood learning—a much more challenging and complicated task that we'll tackle in the following chapter.

Given that core beliefs are tougher to shift than automatic thoughts, one of the best ways to start chipping away at them is to link your most tenacious red-flag thinking—which you're increasingly more aware of—to the faulty conclusions you've made about your ex so we can challenge them simultaneously. This takes some practice, so let's use Akira's story as an example to illustrate how we're going to do it.

Akira noticed Mike as soon as she arrived at her neighbors' annual holiday party. It wasn't his boyish smile or overly long hair that really caught her attention. It was the fact that he was wearing an ugly sweater without any obvious self-consciousness—complete with flashing light bulbs wrapped around reindeer antlers. After exchanging glances, Mike introduced himself, and an intense flirtation began. Within weeks Akira was smitten. She adored Mike's quick wit, sense of humor, self-confidence, and ambition. Life was more fun when they were together; they both liked sushi, going to comedy clubs, and sci-fi movies. And their sex life was incredible. But they were also very different. Mike was outgoing and belonged to a handful of co-ed sports teams that headed to the bar after practice many nights a week. Akira was an introvert who preferred cuddling up on the couch with a good book and a cup of chamomile tea to the bar scene. And they had different cultural backgrounds with divergent views on gender roles. Yet their differences also made their relationship more interesting. They even joked about the "crazy party boy" dating the "serious Asian girl."

After a few months, their honeymoon romance started to give way to stark life realities. Mike came to Akira's place drunk after almost all his practices, which concerned her more over time. She also felt increasingly uncomfortable with Mike's interactions with other women after she overheard him talking to a friend about the "new hot girls" on one of his teams. When they argued about it, Akira found it stressful but also enjoyed the makeup sex. Yet Akira's behavior indicated that she was feeling increasingly uncomfortable. She started going to Mike's games wearing more revealing clothes, and sometimes she went to the bar with him after his practices even though she had to skip her favorite yoga class to do it. Despite these struggles, Akira believed they were meant to be together and saw their conflicts as normal because "all couples have problems."

After about nine months together, Mike told Akira that he didn't want to be with her anymore because she'd changed; she'd become clingy and "didn't accept him as he is." Akira couldn't believe the relative ease with which Mike wished her the best and said he hoped they could be friends. She quickly found herself stuck in the exaholic cycle. Consumed by thoughts of Mike, she desperately wanted to get back together and felt emotionally traumatized by their breakup.

Looking at her self-monitoring logs, Akira's most stubborn automatic thoughts were *I'm nothing without Mike, He never loved me because he wouldn't have left me like this if he did,* and *If he doesn't want me, no one will.* As you can hopefully see easily, all of these are red-flag thoughts; none is accurate or helpful. Yet as much as Akira rationally knew her thinking was flawed, she still felt as though these statements were true. Suspecting that they were being fueled by some faulty core beliefs, we dug deeper and discovered that Akira believed Mike was perfect for her and put him on a pedestal. To maintain those beliefs about him, she often brushed aside things she didn't like, including how much he drank and his comments about other women. When they did fight about these issues, Akira told herself that he would change and interpreted the tension as a reflection of how much they loved each other. At some deep level, she also believed that she needed Mike to be happy and that without him she is less valuable as a person.

As she started understanding her own patterns, Akira practiced linking her red-flag thoughts to the faulty core beliefs that were supporting them:

Stubborn red-flag thought: *I'm nothing without Mike.*

Faulty beliefs that drive this thought: This stems from my belief that Mike's the best. I'm overvaluing him and his opinion of me, as though he defines my value and I need him in order to be complete, whole, and happy.

Stubborn red-flag thought: *He never loved me because he wouldn't have left me like this.*

Faulty beliefs that drive this thought: This stems from a flawed belief that love is enough to make a relationship work. I'm also mistakenly concluding that his choices are personal attacks on me that erase our past connection instead of seeing them as a reflection of who he is and what he wants now.

Stubborn red-flag thought: *If he doesn't want me, no one will.*

Faulty beliefs that drive this thought: This is touching on my flawed belief that Mike's opinion defines me—as though I don't have value or won't meet another romantic partner because Mike doesn't want me.

Stubborn red-flag thought: *Fighting reflects how deeply we love each other.*

Faulty beliefs that drive this thought: This stems from my belief that the highs and lows of fighting reflect love.

When you look at Akira's thinking patterns, you can hopefully see how her faulty beliefs about Mike support and encourage her stubborn red-flag thinking. In addition, Akira felt increasingly insecure over time, even though she wasn't aware of what she was doing and why: she started wearing more revealing clothes to get his attention and gave up activities she enjoyed, like yoga. As Akira learned to identify her faulty beliefs about Mike and saw their effects on her thinking, behaviors, and emotions, not only was it easier for her to challenge her red-flag thoughts in the moment but also to make her beliefs about Mike more accurate and helpful over time.

Shifting your own narrative about your ex by seeing some of the fundamentally flawed beliefs you hold about them can change your entire experience of your breakup. Chipping away at the deceptive fantasy of who your ex is in your own mind will help you let go and move on.

EXERCISE: Linking Red-Flag Thoughts to Faulty Beliefs

As Akira did, you're going to try to link your red-flag thoughts to their corresponding faulty beliefs. Start by writing down your most stubborn red-flag thoughts in your journal. Next, try to identify any faulty core beliefs about your ex that're fueling them. For example, if your red-flag thought is *I'll never find anyone as wonderful as my ex*, it may be coming from a core belief that your ex is the best. If your red-flag thought is *I can't live without my ex*, it may be coming from a flawed core belief that to be complete you need your ex, and that they define your value. Go through your list and link as many stubborn red-flag thoughts to their corresponding faulty core beliefs as you can. Record this exercise as a self-care intervention in your log.

As you look at your faulty core beliefs about your ex, you're hopefully starting to really see how your thinking about them is flawed. As important as this is to your healing journey, it also may leave you wondering *What's actually true about my ex and my former relationship?* Although the answer will be very specific to you, I want to remind you of some fundamental Truths about you and your breakup that can help you build a more self-enhancing, honest worldview moving forward. Embracing these beliefs will also help you rebuild your self-esteem, making it easier to let go of your ex and move on.

Embracing the Truth About Your Breakup

When it comes to faulty beliefs about your ex and this breakup, your ultimate goal is to replace the beliefs with accurate Truths about human nature (Ellis and Harper 1997). I refer to these Truths with a capital *T* because they're essential realities about people. As such, they're true for all of us! So, as often as you can, remind yourself of the following:

- You're just as valuable on your own as you were with your ex.

- Your ex isn't perfect or perfect for you, at least not today.

- Your ex and their opinions of you don't determine your value or desirability—and they never did.

- You're powerless over your ex; you can't make them love or want you.

- You can't change your ex; only they can choose to do that.

- You're a separate person from your ex, each with your own backgrounds, identities, goals, and experiences, and you don't need them to survive.

- You don't need to be with your ex to have a fulfilling present or future.

- You have the power to change your life by making different choices.

Whenever you're battling inaccurate and unhelpful beliefs about your ex or your breakup—like you need your ex to be complete, they're perfect for you, and love is enough to make your relationship work—replace them with one or more of these Truths.

One great way to start integrating them into your worldview is to use the 3 Ds on your faulty beliefs. Just as you did with your automatic thoughts, *detect* the faulty beliefs using the list you came up with earlier; *debate* them, looking for evidence that they're true or false; and *discriminate* what's true and untrue, making your thinking healthier and more accurate using the Truths above. Then see whether your symptoms improve.

Let's use Akira's faulty beliefs about Mike to illustrate this process. As you may remember, Akira believed that Mike was the best, was perfect for her, and made her complete. She also believed that love was enough to make a relationship work and that their fighting reflected how much he loved her. When Akira applied the 3 Ds to her faulty beliefs, it looked like this:

Detect faulty beliefs:

Mike's the best; he's the only man for me. I need him in my life to be complete and fulfilled. Love is enough to make a relationship work. Fighting reflects how much we love each other.

Debate faulty beliefs:

Evidence that these beliefs are true:

Mike's the only person I've ever felt this way about. It was a special connection that I may never find again.

Evidence that these beliefs are false:

Mike's just a person, with faults like the rest of us. He isn't perfect. No one is.

Given that we broke up, Mike isn't perfect for me.

I have just as much value on my own as I did when I was dating Mike.

Mike's desire to be with me, or lack thereof, doesn't define my desirability as a person.

I don't need Mike to be complete. I may miss and want him, but I'm okay alone.

I've dated other people who really liked me, so there are probably other men who will want me in the future.

Love isn't enough to make our relationship work.

Drama isn't the same as love.

I always have myself. I'm enough on my own.

Discriminate (create more accurate and helpful beliefs):

Although this breakup is incredibly difficult for me to accept, I don't need Mike for me to be whole and healed. Mike clearly isn't perfect for me because our relationship didn't work for him. The chaos our fights created doesn't reflect our love; it reflects that we couldn't communicate effectively or reconcile our differences. I'm not doomed to be alone and unhappy forever. I can create a fulfilling future by making healing choices for myself today, and I'm committed to doing so because I want to enjoy my life again.

The more Akira integrated healthier Truths about herself and Mike into her belief system, the more honest and self-enhancing her worldview became over time. So, let's incorporate these Truths into your thinking now.

EXERCISE: Shifting Your Faulty Beliefs

As Akira did, practice using the 3 Ds on your faulty beliefs. Swapping them out for more accurate Truths may feel hard at first because your deeply formed beliefs about your ex can have a real pull on you, but the more you remind yourself of these Truths, the easier it'll become to integrate them into your perspective on your breakup. Over time, you'll come to *know* they're true because they'll organically become a part of your life philosophy. Note your efforts in your log as a self-care intervention.

Moving Forward

It can be mind-blowing when you come to see how much your experiences are shaped by your thinking and beliefs—how the way you think about your ex and this breakup strongly influences the severity and intensity of your exaholic symptoms. Your ultimate goal for doing this work is to emerge from this breakup with a more honest, self-valuing worldview that leaves you with a deep appreciation for your ex, yourself, and this experience. Using the 3 Ds on your red-flag thoughts and faulty beliefs will help you embrace healthier fundamental Truths about yourself—namely that you are valuable, are lovable, and have the power to shape your experience of life. These Truths will help you heal.

What you believe about your ex is so important to letting them go that we need to explore core beliefs at the very deepest level. Although it may sound odd, you started forming your foundational core beliefs about love as a young child. In the next chapter, we'll explore how they predispose you to struggle with love addiction as an adult.

CHAPTER 6

Harmful Childhood Learning About Love

It's been three years since I last spoke to my ex. As I go through this journey of recovery, my symptoms are getting better, but sometimes I worry that something's wrong with me—that I'm somehow incapable of having a healthy relationship. When I meet someone I like, I overanalyze everything. It's like I become extra sensitive to what they say or do. Then I miss my ex more. Why am I like that? I don't know why relationships are so hard for me.

From the time I was a kid, I dreamed about my wedding. It would be outside in a garden of sweet-smelling pink, yellow, and orange flowers. Waiting for me at a greenery-covered altar would be my perfect mate. I would be his everything and he would be mine. With him by my side, my life would fall into place and I'd be happy. I thought my ex was the one. Instead, I fell in love and he didn't. This wasn't part of my dream. Maybe it was always a fantasy.

As I look at my logs, what's clear is that I'm so jaded. I think people are selfish and disappointing. Is it even possible to have a real, trustworthy connection to a lover? If it is, I've never seen it. I guess I don't really know what a healthy romance looks like.

It's natural to think that your exaholic symptoms solely reflect your current relationship situation—that you met your ex, connected, broke up, and entered a state of breakup misery. Yet as the stories above suggest, your reaction to this breakup is highly influenced by conclusions you started making about romantic relationships long before you met your ex. From the time you were born, opened your eyes, peered into your environment, and started learning, what you've concluded about yourself, other people, and the world around you has become the unconscious lens through which you see your life (A. T. Beck 1976; A. T. Beck et al. 1979; J. S. Beck 2021). These foundational core beliefs that developed in early childhood profoundly affect the way you think, feel, and act toward your ex—both when you were together and now that you've broken up (Young et al. 2019). If you don't change them, not only will they keep you stuck on your ex, but they'll also predispose you to exaholic tendencies in future relationships.

Core beliefs about love stemming from early childhood learning are probably the most challenging to become aware of, to assess, and to change because they're the ocean in which your iceberg of faulty beliefs and red-flag thoughts about your ex floats. Yet they perhaps have the most influence on your addictive symptoms because they form the lens through which you experience romantic relationships as an adult (Young, Klosko, and Weishaar 2003; Young et al. 2019). To get over your ex and ward off addictive tendencies with new lovers, you've got to uncover your beliefs about love itself that feed your addiction.

Developing Core Beliefs About Love

Most of us think of love as a deep feeling of care for another person. It reflects affection, adoration, and concern for their well-being (Tobore 2020). But love is actually much more than a feeling; love's *a need*. It's a *drive*. It's the profound experience of emotional care, commitment, and devotion that bonds you to another person and helps us survive as a species (Fisher 2004; Fisher 2016). In these ways love isn't particularly rational. Love is deeply ingrained in the fibers of our being. You can tell me the qualities you love the most about others, but your words will never fully capture or explain your experience. You can also really dislike someone you love deeply; our drive for love is far greater than our rational minds can comprehend.

To really grasp the magnitude of our need for love, consider human babies. When we're born, we can't meet our own basic needs. We need someone to feed us, clean us, hold us, and keep us safe from harm. Essentially, *we need someone to love us*. Without it, we can't thrive or even survive. It's love that compels most parents to take care of their kids. And it's also love that motivates us to connect to and bond with others. In fact, many of us would die for those we love the most, and some even kill in the name of love, which shows just how powerful this basic human drive can be (Fisher 2016; Harlow 1958).

Given our profound need for love, the degree to which you felt loved—safe, valued, cared for, understood, accepted—as a child dramatically influences your core beliefs about yourself and others in relationships. You were born into a family, a country, a culture, and a historical time that served as the environmental foundation for your growth and development. Like a sponge, you absorbed everything you saw—and you started *learning*. You learned by copying what other people were doing, modeling the behavior of your parents, siblings, and friends (Bandura 1977). You learned by seeing how people responded to you—whether they applauded or disliked your actions (Skinner 1974). You learned by observing the characteristics that made people look good or bad in your cultural context (Sue and Sue 2012; Warren and Akoury 2020). Everything around you served as a mechanism for learning: how people acted and dressed, what they ate, how they talked, how they treated each other, and what they expected from others in romantic relationships.

As shown in figure 2, your family, sociocultural environment, peers, friends, early dating partners, and other unique circumstances served as the breeding ground for your learning as a child. As you observed and interacted with your environment, you developed some foundational core beliefs about yourself and others in loving relationships. These stable, fixed conclusions that developed early in life are reflected in every aspect of your romantic relationship with your ex—what you were attracted to, how safe you felt, how you expected your ex to treat you, how you treated them, and how you expressed love. These, in turn, affected your beliefs about your ex and your red-flag automatic thinking, both when you were together and now that you're broken up.

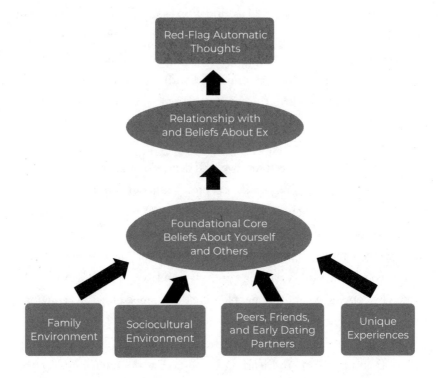

Figure 2: How early childhood learning affects love addiction.

Here's the key to how your early childhood learning affects your romantic relationships, including the one with your ex: *core beliefs that formed when you felt unloved, unsafe, or insecure as a child will make it difficult for you to trust and be close to romantic partners as an adult.* If you didn't receive enough support, guidance, and stability as a child, your core beliefs will reflect that love isn't stable or safe (A. T. Beck et al. 1979; J. S. Beck 2021). If you were hurt in some way, for example, you may have unconsciously concluded that the world's unfair, people will always take advantage of you, and something's wrong with you. Even worse, if you were mistreated, victimized, or traumatized by *adverse childhood experiences* (also referred to as ACEs by mental health professionals)—you were physically abused, were sexually mistreated, were neglected, saw domestic violence, lived in a household with substance abuse, had a parent with a severe mental illness, or witnessed a messy divorce—you're especially likely to struggle in romantic relationships now (Anda et al. 2006; Francoeur et al. 2020; Heshmati, Zemestani, and Vujanovic 2021; Hughes et al. 2017). You may even have concluded that you are not fully lovable, don't have inherent value on your own, and have no control over what happens to you in life (J. S. Beck 2021). Adverse childhood experiences can even change your physiological responses to stress, thereby warping your reactions to difficult life events, like this breakup (Filbey 2019; Van der Watt et al. 2021).

As we wade into the murky waters of your childhood learning, you're probably going to be reminded of some unpleasant memories, because it's those negative experiences that affect your addiction to your ex the most. If that happens, try to become an observer of yourself. Detach from the memories enough to see the larger picture of what you learned from any traumatic, damaging, or abusive events without reexperiencing them. As you look back, ask yourself *what your childhood environment taught you about yourself and others*. Your answer will lead you to your most influential core beliefs. Remember that you didn't consciously choose your beliefs as a child; you unconsciously drew these conclusions through your experiences. Let's start with perhaps the most important influence on your learning: your family.

Family Messages About Love

Your family members are the first and probably most developmentally important people you'll encounter in life (Ainsworth 1989; Bowlby 1971; Harlow 1958). You learned your earliest life lessons and formed your first bonds (or didn't) with your family because you needed their love to survive. In addition, you probably spent most of your time with your family as a child, a developmental phase when we're most vulnerable to the influence of other people because we don't have a clear identity apart from our adult caregivers (Kail and Cavanaugh 2010).

Research pioneered in the 1960s and '70s describes how interactions with family—particularly parents—affect how comfortable you are being close to and emotionally bonded to others (Ainsworth 1989; Bowlby 1975; Bretherton 1992). If you were able to depend on your parents to meet your needs—thereby experiencing healthy expressions of parental love—you're likely to become *securely attached* or bonded to them in a healthy way. In an ideal childhood environment, that's exactly what happens. You learn that your parents will help you and take care of you. That they come back after they leave. That you're safe and free to explore your world, returning to your parents for support, comfort, and reassurance anytime you need it because they'll always be there. In this kind of family environment, you develop core beliefs that reflect you are valuable, are safe, and have the power to influence your own life. As an adult, it's relatively easy for you to develop close and meaningful romantic relationships because your core beliefs reflect that you are important, are secure, and can effectively maneuver through whatever challenges life throws your way (Bretherton 1992; Hazan and Shafer 1987; Levine and Heller 2012; Mellody, Miller, and Miller 2003).

As nice as that family situation sounds, many of us didn't grow up in such an idyllic environment. If your parents responded inconsistently to your needs—sometimes they were there for you and sometimes not—you're more likely to be *anxiously attached* to others now. This leaves you craving intimacy but preoccupied by your relationships and uncertain of people's ability to love you because you were never sure whether your adult caregivers would be there for you or not. If your parents were consistently distant or unresponsive to your needs, you're more likely to be *avoidantly attached* now, feeling suffocated by closeness and seeing intimacy as a loss of independence. If your parents were available sometimes and distant at other times, you may have developed a combination of the styles describe above, referred to as a *disorganized attachment* style. This can leave you seeking intimacy at times while actively rejecting it at other times, as if you're clingy in some situations and rejecting in others.

The degree to which you felt loved by your parents and family dramatically affects how you think, feel, and act in your romantic relationships

(Hazan and Shafer 1987; Levine and Heller 2012; Van der Watt et al. 2021). So, let's take a closer look at your experiences.

EXERCISE: Your Family Learning About Love

In your journal, reflect on your childhood family learning. Start by describing who was in your family, which can include anyone who helped raise you, lived with you, or spent a lot of time in your childhood environment. This list often includes biological or adoptive parents, grandparents, siblings, cousins, and even members of your extended family or pets. Your list should also include people who you wanted to connect with but didn't because they were absent from your life because they died, were incarcerated, lived far away, or simply didn't make an effort, for example.

Then describe your family environment. Where did you live and who lived with you? What did your household feel like? Was it chaotic or calm? Were your parents physically and emotionally available? Did they support and validate your experiences? Did you feel safe? How did people talk to and treat each other? Handle conflict and disagreements? Were there expectations about how you needed to look or act to be loved? Did anyone struggle with addiction or another mental health condition? Were you ever mistreated or abused? Describe anything noteworthy about your childhood family environment.

Now, looking at what you wrote, ask yourself this question: *What did I learn about myself and others from my family environment?* Some common core beliefs born from difficult early childhood family systems include:

- I'm unlovable.

- I'm broken; something's wrong with me.

- I'm not safe.

- I'm bad.

- Love is conditional. It must be earned.

- People aren't trustworthy.

- People will always leave me.

- Relationships are dangerous.

Do any of these core beliefs resonate with you? Did you make any other conclusions about love because of your family environment? It's important to note that your experiences may have led you to draw *negative and accurate* conclusions about other people. If you lived through more extreme adverse childhood experiences like abuse, you may have reasonably concluded that *People aren't trustworthy.* It makes logical sense for a child who's being abused to develop that belief. In these situations, what's important to remember is that your conclusions aren't completely true now: some people aren't trustworthy but many are, and as an adult you can choose who's in your life. So, continuing to hold on to this core belief, or any of the others noted so far, doesn't serve you well.

In addition, you may have drawn conclusions that were fundamentally untrue even as a child, but you believed they were true. For example, if you were neglected and concluded *Something's wrong with me—I'm unlovable,* that's simply not true and never was. If you see red-flag thinking in your childhood core beliefs, remind yourself that your conclusions aren't accurate or helpful, even if it makes sense that you believed them when you were young.

In addition to the beliefs you formed in your family environment, you were raised in a cultural context. So, next we're going to examine what your sociocultural surroundings taught you.

Cultural Messages About Love

All of us were born into a culture, a social group that shares specific values, norms, customs, and rules (Schwartz 1992; Sue and Sue 2012). In fact, you belong or belonged to many cultural groups. Some may have been smaller, like being a member of your neighborhood or church, whereas others were much larger, like being part of an ethnic group or nation. Each cultural group you encounter holds specific values about what makes people lovable and esteemed from a social perspective—everything from character traits, like being kind and friendly, to demographic characteristics, like race, sex, sexual orientation, gender, class, financial status, education, and physical beauty (Sue and Sue 2012; Warren and Akoury 2020).

As a child, you learned the values and ideals of your cultures simply by living in them—watching television, interacting with media, observing the power structures of organizations, being taught in school, and identifying who had the most power in your community and why (Sue and Sue 2012). You learned what's normal, desirable, and reasonable to expect in romantic relationships within your cultural contexts, so dissecting the messaging you received is key to understanding your love addiction. If you grew up in a first-world Western environment, for example, many of the strongest messages about romance present a highly unrealistic Cinderella and Prince Charming story. People in this cultural context are taught that when you find your one and only true love, they'll fall for you, want you, and fight to be with you, and you'll live happily ever after. To be desirable, you should strive to be wealthy, be fit, be smart, be straight, be beautiful or handsome, and stay looking youthful forever (Warren and Akoury 2020). If you grew up in a more collectivistic context in which the needs of the community are put above individual desires, you may have learned that your job is to ensure the well-being of your family and community over your own personal love interests (Regan, Lakhanpal, and Anguiano 2012). All of this is to say that when considering potential lovers, you may evaluate them from the perspective of your family rather than your own. For example, if you grew up in a rigidly religious community, you may have learned that you should only date people who hold the same spiritual beliefs or should feel guilty for any sexual thoughts that are viewed as impure (Miller 1999).

The cultural messages you internalized as a child are profoundly important because you unconsciously believed them to be true without considering whether they're accurate, attainable, or even healthy. We rarely see real, raw depictions of lasting intimate romantic relationships in the media or through other cultural communications, such as in television shows, movies, open community dialogue about relationship struggles, or conversations about infidelity. As a result, you may hold the core belief that someone who loves you never thinks about having sexual or romantic relationships with other people. Or doubts their marital choices. Or struggles to be close to you. You may believe that loving couples never fight, or that it's normal to have passionate blowouts followed by the silent treatment and over-the-top gestures of reuniting! Or that something's wrong with you if you are not straight, don't look perfect, are single, or are rejected by a lover. Clearly, these beliefs aren't true or healthy for any of us.

EXERCISE: Your Cultural Learning About Love

In your journal, reflect on your childhood cultural learning. How would you describe the culture or cultures you grew up in? What made someone valuable? Who was most loved? Why were they loved? Is it important to be married? Beautiful or handsome? Smart? Financially successful? Independent and self-sufficient? How are breakups and divorce viewed? Should people act a certain way based on their sex or gender? Consider what made someone valuable, insignificant, or socially ostracized in your cultural contexts.

Next, ask yourself what these contexts taught you about yourself and others in romantic relationships. Some common untrue core beliefs that can emerge from unrealistic or unhealthy cultural messages about love include:

- In romantic relationships, two people become one.

- I have only one true love.

- I can't be whole or happy without a partner.

- My value depends on external factors, like how much money I have and how pretty I look.

- I must be better than other people to find and keep a mate.

- I'll disgrace my community if my relationship fails.

Elaborate on these or other core beliefs that you learned from your cultural contexts.

Next, we turn our attention to the third major influence on your childhood learning: peers, friends, and early dating experiences.

Peer Messages About Love

From childhood into adolescence, peer-group and dating relationships become increasingly important and influential (Ainsworth 1989; American Psychological Association 2002). As humans, we're social beings. We need interpersonal relationships to feel connected to others, have fun, and survive (Kail and Cavanaugh 2010). Especially as a child, we want to belong to a peer group and be accepted by our similarly-aged friends. Rejection, bullying, and social ostracization often leave us feeling unlovable. In addition, during this phase we're forming our identify amongst our peers, exploring our individuality, autonomy, and sexuality (American Psychological Association 2002). To figure out who we are, we need interactions with others—even difficult ones.

Given our social nature, early experiences with peers, friends, and dating partners strongly influenced your foundational core beliefs about love and romantic relationships. As a child, you watched how your peers and friends acted in school. You saw how they treated you and compared yourself to them to see where you fit in. You explored your earliest same-age sexual and romantic curiosities around them—feeling your first crushes and exploring how to dress or act in a flirtatious way. You also started developing beliefs about how lovers should act, and when, how, and with whom it's appropriate for people in your peer group to be sexual (American Psychological Association 2002). As you moved into adolescence, you may have had your first dating or sexual experiences within your peer group, and whether they were pleasant, fun, terrible, scary, traumatic, or awkward affected your view of romantic love as you aged (Halpern-Meekin et al. 2013; Francoeur et al. 2020; O'Sullivan et al. 2019).

EXERCISE: Peer and Early Dating Learning About Love

Going back to your journal, reflect on your childhood peer-group learning. Start by thinking about your peers—people who weren't necessarily your friends but were about your age and in your grade or social environment. How would you describe yourself in relation to them growing up? Did you fit in? What influenced who was most popular or most well-liked? Do you have any specific memories of difficult interactions with your peers? Did someone bully you or treat you disrespectfully?

Next, think about your friends. Did you have close friends growing up? Did you have a best friend? Did you trust and confide in them? How did they express love and affection? Did you ever have a falling-out with one of your friends? Why and how did it affect you? When did your friends start having sexual interactions? Did they use pornography? Did they believe in monogamy or embrace a more open view of sexuality and romance?

Finally, think about your early dating experiences. Who was the first person you had a crush on? How would you describe them? What did you like about them? Did they like you back? What are some common characteristics of people you're attracted to? Have you had any particularly positive or negative dating experiences? When was your first sexual experience and how did it unfold? When did you first notice feeling addicted to a love interest? If you've felt addicted to dating partners in addition to your ex, describe them and your experience.

As you look at what you wrote about your peers, friends, and early dating experiences, ask yourself what you learned from them. Some common core beliefs that can emerge as a result of feeling insecure, uncomfortable, or unwanted include:

- I'm not as good as other people.

- I have to make people like me to be valuable.

- Being close to people is dangerous.

- Men will always use and abuse me.

- Women will always use and abuse me.

- Lovers always cheat.

Finally, we're going to consider any unique experiences that affected your comfort in intimate relationships.

Learning Unique to You

Growing up, each of us had unique experiences that made a strong impression and affected us deeply and shaped our view of love and relationships. It could be that someone you really loved died. That you were adopted. That you had a sibling with special needs. That you were raised in a military or strictly religious family. That you experienced racism or sexism in a highly damaging way. That you were a refugee and struggled to acculturate to your new environment. That you had an influential travel experience. That you were in a car accident or had a severe physical illness. That you were assaulted or attacked. That you lived through a natural disaster. That you were a very good or bad student in school. That you have a disability of some kind. The options are endless.

Any experience that taught you something about your own self-worth, or about what to expect from others who claim to love you, can be useful to understanding your core beliefs. So, let's try to identify your unique learnings.

EXERCISE: Unique Situations That Taught You About Love

In your journal, describe your unique childhood learning. Remember that beliefs formed from unsafe or traumatic experiences strongly affect how you experience romantic relationships. So, think about any difficult events or realities you experienced. Although it's hard for me to help you target core beliefs related to unique situations because the possibilities are diverse, here are some general core beliefs that can emerge:

- No one will ever understand or accept me.

- I can't keep myself safe.

- I must be better than others to survive.

- People will always use me to benefit themselves.

- The world is a scary place.

- Don't let people see the real you because they'll reject you.

These foundational core beliefs you formed interacting with your family, sociocultural environment, peers, friends, dating partners, and other unique situations as a child strongly affect your addiction to your ex. To start discerning the complicated nuances of how, we're going to take on the difficult task of linking your childhood core beliefs to your relationship with your ex.

Core Beliefs That Fuel Love Addiction

As you're uncovering through this work, your upbringing led you to develop some foundational core beliefs about yourself and others in relationships (A. T. Beck et al. 1979; J. S. Beck 2021). If as a child you doubted your lovability, safety, and ability to control the direction of your life, the core beliefs that developed as a result will make it difficult for you to trust and be close to romantic partners (Hazan and Shafer 1987; Levine and Heller 2012; Van der Watt et al. 2021; Young et al. 2019). Any version of *I'm not valuable*, *I'm unsafe*, or *I'm powerless* affected your relationship with your ex and needs to be changed (A. T. Beck et al. 1979; J. S. Beck 2021). But connecting your foundational childhood core beliefs to your love addiction is challenging, so we're going to start with an example to guide you through this process. Let's consider Sofia's story.

Sofia was the youngest of three girls born into a working-class second-generation European American family. She described her family environment as tense; yelling and name-calling often filled the air late at night when she was supposed to be asleep. Sofia vividly remembers anxiously sitting on the marker-stained couch in her living room as her father told her that he was moving out. She was seven years old and her parents were divorcing.

After her parents split up, Sofia and her sisters lived with their mother. Sofia described her mom as a tough, hardworking woman who did the best she could to take care of her: she worked two jobs and was chronically tired but rarely showed emotion. Sometimes Sofia would catch her mom weeping softly as she washed dishes late at night, but she never talked to her about it. Sofia rarely saw her dad. She remembers many occasions of waiting excitedly by her living room window for him to pick her up, suitcase in hand, but he rarely came.

In her culture and community, Sofia learned that she needed to be pretty and smart, and that she had to go to church to be a "good girl." Throughout her childhood and teenage years, Sofia did well in school, tried to look nice, attended church, and was never in trouble. In fact, she rarely expressed negative emotions for fear she wouldn't be accepted or liked. Sofia was seen as shy, observant and cautious of her peers, and wary of boys; older kids, parties, and people drinking made her very uncomfortable. Other than her best friend, Sofia didn't have many social outlets. When Sofia was eleven, her oldest sister got pregnant out of wedlock, which upset her mother and further solidified Sofia's trepidation around men.

After graduating from high school and working for a few years, Sofia met Malik at a coffee shop. Initially she brushed him off, as she did most men, but he was persistent. One morning after ordering her usual coffee, the barista smiled and handed her a cup with a note from Malik: "I'd love to get to know you." Thinking his gesture was cute, Sofia agreed to go on a date. Much to her surprise, she enjoyed being around Malik. He was attentive, good-looking, and very interested in her. Within a month, Sofia started to let down her guard—and she felt incredible! She felt complete and happy with him by her side and thought her life was finally coming together. But Sofia was also increasingly anxious when they were apart and, over time, became overly focused on the details of Malik's behavior: how often he called, the specific words he used when he talked to her, and how much time passed between texts. She wanted constant reassurance that he loved her and that they were seriously pursuing a future together.

After a few months of dating, Malik's demeanor started to shift. When Sofia wanted more attention, Malik pulled back. He stopped sending her sweet messages, didn't make as much of an effort to spend time with her, and seemed irritated with her. When Sofia tried to talk to him about how she felt, Malik said she was getting crazy. Soon, they broke up and Sofia became mired in the exaholic cycle. Consumed by obsessive thinking, deeply upsetting emotions, and cravings to be with him, she felt utterly lost and betrayed. When she shared her story about Malik with her family, Sofia's mom rolled her eyes and said, "That's just how men are."

Do you see how Sofia's family, culture, peers, and unique experiences led to conclusions about love that influenced her relationship and exaholic breakup with Malik? Unpacking how early childhood core beliefs affect adult relationship patterns is challenging, so let's break her story down together.

Looking at her family learning, we can see that Sofia wasn't securely attached to either of her parents: her mother was physically present but emotionally distant, while her father was not actively a part of her life after age seven. This caused Sofia to be wary of intimacy and of trusting others. She also erroneously believed that something was wrong with her—that if she were more perfect, her mom would be happier and her dad would want to have a relationship with her. Culturally, Sofia unconsciously internalized the belief that if she were perfect—a good daughter who is pretty and smart and never gets in trouble—then good things would happen to her. So, she didn't express any negative emotions for fear that it would make her look bad. Socially, Sofia was wary of getting close to people: she trusted her best friend but had few other social contacts in her peer group. Sofia avoided romantic relationships during adolescence because men had left the women in her life, including herself, her mother, and her sister. Feeling abandoned by her father and seeing her sister get pregnant further solidified her distrust.

Here are the foundational core beliefs that Sofia identified:

- Something's wrong with me. If I were better—smarter, prettier, nicer, more lovable—people would love me.

- Men are selfish; they'll use you and then leave.

- Romantic love is dangerous.

- People aren't trustworthy.

Given the fundamental core beliefs about love that Sofia developed in childhood, it's not surprising that falling in love with Malik brought out her insecurities and vulnerabilities in ways that hurt their relationship. Unconsciously, Sofia believed that romantic love was dangerous and that men would always leave her. So, Sofia didn't really date anyone through adolescence and avoided romantic relationships until Malik seduced her into getting to know him. As Malik pursued her and showered her with positive attention, Sofia started to let him in. As she fell in love, she felt wonderful and concluded that he was the best—an exception to the men she'd known and the perfect partner for her. She erroneously believed that as long as they were together, she'd be safe and happy. Yet, as we explored in the last chapter, these are common yet highly faulty beliefs we make about our lover when we fall in love because it feels so good to be around them, and because we put them on a pedestal.

Over time, Sofia became more and more uncomfortable being close to Malik, in part because her childhood core beliefs were activated. Unconsciously, she worried that Malik would uncover the truth that something's wrong with her (even though that's clearly objectively false!) and felt increasingly desperate for reassurance that he wasn't going to leave her, which Malik found exhausting, suffocating, and unattractive. In essence, Sofia's relationship with Malik triggered some profoundly deep, dark pain from her childhood: her core beliefs kept her from feeling safe, valued, and in control of herself in her relationship. Even before their breakup, her beliefs began to erode their connection because Malik couldn't make her feel safe no matter what he did: Sofia believed that romantic love was dangerous, people would always leave her, men would use her, and she was fundamentally broken as a person. Ultimately, Sofia's core beliefs created discord in the relationship both before and after they broke up. They also fueled Sofia's symptoms of love addiction because she unconsciously saw their breakup as evidence that her negative childhood core beliefs were true (J. S. Beck 2021), which further ignited red-flag thinking that inflamed her exaholic cycle.

As you can hopefully see from Sofia's story, connecting your childhood learning to your exaholic breakup is messy and complicated. And yet doing so is critical to letting go of your ex and creating a future free of love addiction. So, let's try to connect the dots between your childhood core beliefs about love, faulty beliefs about your ex, and red-flag thinking.

EXERCISE: Linking Childhood Beliefs to Your Breakup

Look at the foundational core beliefs you learned from your family, culture, peers, dating partners, and other unique experiences in childhood. Then, try to pinpoint how they affected your thoughts, feelings, and behaviors related to your relationship with your ex. While you were together and after you broke up, which of your beliefs emerged? Can you see how your beliefs seeped into the way you interacted with your ex, as Sofia's beliefs did for her? Did you trust your ex? Did you feel comfortable being close to them? Some common ways that difficult childhood learning can affect love-addicted relationships and breakups include:

- Wanting to bond too quickly, or feeling suffocated when your partner wants to be close.

- Feeling very sensitive to your partner's likes, opinions, and moods.

- Worrying that your romantic partner will stop loving you.

- Worrying that your romantic partner will leave you (even if you rationally don't really like them or want to be with them).

- Paying careful attention to every aspect of what your partner is or isn't doing (for example, how often they communicate with you or the specific words they use).

- Wanting regular reassurance of your partner's love and devotion, or bristling when your partner wants too many affirmations from you.

- Feeling uncomfortable being vulnerable because you're afraid your partner will reject you.

- Becoming easily triggered or reactive when your partner doesn't respond the way you want.

- Hiding or trying to disguise negative things about your-self because you're afraid of being judged.

- Feeling uncomfortable when you're away from your partner.

- Feeling competitive with other people who threaten to take away your partner's attention.

- Struggling to leave relationships even when they're unhealthy.

- Feeling incomplete or lost when you're not in a relationship.

> Do you experience romantic relationships in any of these ways? Were you this way with your ex? Pause to identify and remember specific examples of how these tendencies emerged in your relationship with your ex when you were together and now that you're broken up. Record your efforts as a self-care intervention in your log.

As you become more aware of your faulty core beliefs that developed in childhood and how they fuel your addiction to your ex, you'll start to understand how important it is to change them! Specifically, you'll want to replace them with healthier, more accurate and helpful Truths about yourself, others, and romantic relationships.

Healthier Beliefs About You and Romantic Relationships

Unfortunately for all of us, many of the most harmful and untrue core beliefs we learned in childhood become stronger over the course of our lives because we unintentionally reinforce and maintain them (Van der Watt et al. 2021). We do this by paying more attention to evidence that supports them being true, acting in ways consistent with them being true, and discounting evidence that they're false or don't serve us well anymore (J. S. Beck 2021; Starcke et al. 2018). For example, Sofia's own behavior—the result of her core beliefs about love and romance—may have elicited the very outcome she feared most: Malik leaving her. When he did leave, she unknowingly interpreted it as evidence that her core beliefs were true; that men would always leave her, she is broken, and relationships are dangerous.

So, core beliefs formed in early childhood are particularly hard to challenge because you've unintentionally been reinforcing them for years (O'Sullivan et al. 2019).

To develop a more self-enhancing belief system, you'll need to replace your unhelpful childhood core beliefs with more honest Truths about you, your ex, and love. You started integrating some of these Truths into your worldview in the last chapter, but we're going to build on that work by focusing on your inherent value as a person. When you notice a flawed and harmful childhood belief emerge in your thoughts, behaviors, and actions, I want you to remind yourself of the following:

- I'm lovable.

- I'm valuable just as I am.

- I don't need the approval of my ex to be important.

- I don't need to meet cultural ideals to be valuable.

- I don't need to be in a relationship to be safe and secure in my own skin.

- Being in a romantic relationship is a choice. I don't need a partner to be complete.

- I have the power to change my life through my choices.

Some of these statements may feel hokey or even false to you right now, but the reality is that they reflect the Truth for each one of us. Anytime you see a faulty childhood core belief driving your exaholic symptoms, I want you to replace it with one of these fundamental Truths (Ellis and Harper 1997). Let's practice doing that now.

EXERCISE: Shifting Your Childhood Core Beliefs

Practice using the 3 Ds to challenge your childhood core beliefs. We'll use Sofia as an example to get you started.

Detect faulty childhood core beliefs:

If I were better—smarter, prettier, nicer—people would love me and want me in their life. Something's wrong with me. Men are selfish; they'll use me and leave me. Romantic love is dangerous.

Debate:

Evidence that core beliefs are true:

My dad and my sister's boyfriend left, leaving my mom and sister to raise their kids alone, which leads me to think men are selfish.

I haven't seen a safe and nurturing romantic relationship, so love seems very dangerous.

Evidence that core beliefs are false:

As an adult, I don't need anyone to take care of me because I can take care of myself.

I don't need a romantic partner to be safe and fulfilled.

My parents' inability to take care of me as a child is not a reflection of my value. Nor is my ex's lack of desire to be with me now.

My past doesn't define my future.

Even if I wasn't securely bonded to my parents, it doesn't mean I can't learn to bond with others now.

If one lover leaves me—as Malik did—it doesn't mean that all men will leave. Not all men are dangerous or irresponsible.

If people leave or don't want me in their life, it doesn't mean something's wrong with me. Other people's behavior and choices are reflections of who they are, not of who I am.

I'm enough just as I am. Even if I'm not perfect, I'm still worthy of love.

No matter what life brings my way, I still have me.

Discriminate (create a more accurate and helpful worldview):

Even though my parents weren't fully available to me when I was a child, that doesn't mean that everyone I love will leave me. I can take care of my own needs now—I don't need anyone to be safe, valuable, and secure. To get over Malik and have better relationships in the future, I need to heal myself from this breakup and change unhelpful core beliefs from my childhood. I'm going to consistently challenge my faulty core beliefs and embrace healthier Truths—that I'm lovable, I'm valuable just as I am, and I don't need the approval of Malik or anyone else to be important. I can change my life through my choices, and I'm doing that now because I want a fulfilling future.

Practice the 3 Ds on all your harmful childhood core beliefs at least once a day, and note your efforts in your self-monitoring log as a self-care intervention.

The more you embrace accurate Truths about yourself and others that come from a place of healthy love, security, and personal empowerment, the better you'll feel both when you're on your own and when you're in romantic relationships. Absorb these Truths and integrate them into your worldview with a deep, inner knowing that they do indeed reflect human nature.

Moving Forward

As a child, you quite literally needed love to survive (Ainsworth 1989; Harlow 1958). What you learned about love early in life affected the degree to which you feel loved, safe, and empowered as an adult. As a child you developed some fundamentally flawed core beliefs that hurt your relationship with your ex because the beliefs made being close to and trusting of others uncomfortable (Young et al. 2019).

Now that you've unearthed some of the harmful childhood core beliefs that make you prone to struggling in romantic relationships—including this one with your ex—it's time to build a brighter future. In part 3 of this book, you're going to learn how to funnel into yourself the energy you've been spending on your ex. You're going to use it to explore who you are and what really matters to you now. As you let go of the pain of the past through forgiveness and by making amends, you can make value-based choices that will lead you to the next great chapter of your life.

Part 3

Choosing Your Next Life

CHAPTER 7

Overcoming Loss Through Forgiveness

When we first broke up, I blamed my ex for everything. Even though I loved him and desperately wanted him back, I also hated him. For leaving. For not wanting me. For moving on so quickly. But exploring my childhood learning helps me see that I added to our relationship issues, too. Growing up in a chaotic household full of tension and unpredictability made it hard for me to trust people. As I understand my own struggles with intimacy, I see that we didn't break up just because of my ex's choices—we also broke up because of mine. Knowing that takes some of the sting out of my wounds.

It's been 231 days since I spoke to my ex. The way she treated me when we broke up was horrible. I felt betrayed and discarded. I'm so bitter at how she handled it. I want to let go of my hurt and anger, but I don't know how. It's eating me up inside.

Over the last five years, I've spent most of my time and energy on my ex—both when we were together and after we broke up. She was the center of my life in my own mind even when I didn't want her to be. As I practice these skills I'm less fixated on her, but it still feels like an enormous loss. Not only the loss of my ex, but also of a part of myself and an old life that's never coming back. It helps me to acknowledge that as I try to move on.

My hope is that you're starting to see the end of your relationship from the broader perspective of your life's journey. Instead of being zoomed in on the painful details of your breakup, you're zooming out to see it as one important part of your much larger story. As if you're fifty feet tall and looking down on a large map of your life from birth until now, you can see that interactions with your family, sociocultural environment, peers, friends, and early dating partners led you to develop some core beliefs about love and relationships. Your most painful and traumatic early childhood experiences led to the most problematic beliefs because what you concluded made it hard for you to be close to others and to trust them (Hazan and Shafer 1987; Levine and Heller 2012). These experiences also probably flooded your young system with stress-induced hormones that shifted your brain chemistry, which continues to influence your physiological reactions to adversity today (Anda et al. 2006; Van der Watt et al. 2021).

Keeping this early learning perspective in mind, move along your winding life map to the day you met your ex. Being around them felt wonderful, leading you to make overly positive conclusions about them—that they were the best, the perfect mate, the one person in the world you needed to feel happy and complete. As you tried to get closer, however, those pesky childhood core beliefs thwarted your experience by making you uncomfortable and by leading you to act in ways consistent with the harmful conclusions you'd already made about yourself and others. After you broke up, you entered a state of love withdrawal, and the exaholic cycle emerged—the obsessive thinking, cravings, emotional distress, and unhealthy acting out—as you tried to feel close to the object of your perceived pain. Taken together, your addiction to your ex developed from a complicated interaction between biological and environmental factors that started long ago but continues to affect you today.

As you see the bigger picture of how you got here and continue to practice CBT skills designed to stop your symptoms, you're actually transforming. Like a phoenix rising from the ashes, you're emerging as a stronger, more authentic version of yourself. Not one who forgets or ignores the past, but one who uses the deeper learning this breakup offers to stretch and grow (Kansky and Allen 2018). Our focus in part 3 of this book is helping you create the next great chapter of your life. The truth is that how you respond to this breakup—whether it's with bitterness and resentment or with compassion and gratitude—will largely determine your enjoyment of moving forward. The more you can accept your breakup as a loss while making amends for your role and choosing to forgive the past, the easier it'll be for you to let go of your ex and start your next adventure. So, we're going to start by looking at this breakup as a grieving process—the internal journey you go through when you lose something that really matters to you (Kübler-Ross 2014). Let's begin.

Grieving the Loss of Your Ex

Even as you get some distance from the daily misery of your symptoms, this breakup probably still feels like a massive loss (Heshmati, Zemestani, and Vujanovic 2021; Reimer and Estrada 2021). It may even feel traumatic, like a death of sorts, because losing your ex isn't just the end a relationship; it's the end of a dream, a lifestyle, a profoundly important connection to a person who once shared your heart, head, and body. When we experience a loss, we *grieve*. Accepting your loss is critical to emerging from grief, and to preventing it from blackening your present and derailing your future (Kübler-Ross 2014). So, let's explore the grieving process in more detail.

When a romantic relationship ends, the grieving process often starts with *shock*—disbelief that your relationship is over and your ex is gone (Kübler-Ross 2014; Reimer and Estrada 2021). During this phase, you may feel numb and disoriented, as though you're living in a terrible dream. Shock is often accompanied by *denial*, which you already know is red-flag thinking that keeps you from honestly admitting to reality. In this phase, you'll internally fight the fact that your relationship is over and search for some acceptable reason why this is happening. You'll yearn to step into an alternative reality in which your ex is still in love with you, wanting you, needing you, making effort to be together—even when none of that's true. Ultimately, denial keeps you holding on to something that's already gone.

After the shock and denial begin to fade, you may enter a phase of *bargaining* in which you frantically try to get back together (Kübler-Ross 2014; Reimer and Estrada 2021). You'll search for ways to fix whatever went wrong in a desperate, last-ditch effort to reunite. You may even consider doing things that you know aren't healthy, violate your moral compass, or hurt your self-esteem. For example, you may convince yourself to be less serious, have an open relationship, give up your dream of having children, financially support your ex, or cut off friends your ex doesn't like simply to get back together. In the end, bargaining puts the responsibility of repairing a relationship that one (or both) of you no longer wants, or isn't healthy, on you.

When you realize that bargaining isn't working—your ex isn't coming back or your relationship can't be repaired in a healthy way—you become flooded with *emotion*. You may feel intense anger or even rage when you think about your breakup (Kübler-Ross 2014; Reimer and Estrada 2021). As the loss of your ex solidifies in your heart and mind, the injustice and senselessness of it all consumes you. You may resent your ex for some of their choices, behaviors, or apparent disregard for your feelings. You may even want to hurt them or make them suffer; these are common reactions to feeling rejected, but ultimately they're not good for you or your relationships (Perilloux and Buss 2008). Flashbacks of other losses or traumas may emerge during this phase that remind you of times you felt unloved, unwanted, or unsafe. Guilt or shame for not behaving as you would have liked and for wishing you could have done things differently—or for believing in a fantasy version of your ex that wasn't real—often accompanies this anger. Underneath it all is profound sadness that your relationship ended and your ex is gone.

As you emerge from the shock, denial, bargaining, and strong emotional phases of grief, the most beautiful thing can happen: you *accept* your loss (Kübler-Ross 2014; Reimer and Estrada 2021). The truth that your relationship ended starts to sink in. You may not like it that your ex is gone or that you're broken up, but you come to see reality for what it is: *you're broken up and you still have a life to live.* You stop wishing you could go back to the way it was and learn to tolerate the painful thoughts, emotions, and bodily sensations that honestly reflect your loss as you look for ways to move on (Hayes, Strosahl, and Wilson 2012). The more you accept your breakup, the easier it becomes to look back at it without such intense reactions (Kübler-Ross 2014). To see that this experience taught you some profoundly important things about yourself that you can use to make different choices moving forward.

Do you resonate with these phases of grief? As you think about how they relate to your experience, let's examine them using Laila's story. Laila started therapy after Anthony, her partner of four years, broke up with her. When she reflected on her breakup as a grieving process, she wrote the following in her journal:

> When Anthony left, I was shocked. I couldn't believe it. It didn't make any sense. I cried and pleaded with him to come back, but he wasn't interested in being a couple anymore. He said we had grown apart and he wanted to move on. Looking back, I was in and out of the denial and bargaining phases for many months. That is, until I learned he was already seriously dating his coworker—then my emotional stages of grief emerged. At first, I was furious. I'd spend hours telling him off in my own head, detailing every way he manipulated me and how much of a liar he was. One night, I ran into them at a party. As I watched him snuggle up to her, I lost it. I walked straight up to them, said some not-so-kind words, threw my drink in his face, and stormed off. Even though it felt good in the moment, ultimately I was embarrassed by the way I acted. Of course, under the anger is just deep sadness that our relationship is over and he doesn't seem to care.
>
> As I use my CBT skills to get some control over my symptoms, I'm moving into the acceptance phase of grief more and more. I'm not in shock anymore. I'm not bargaining. When I'm triggered, I go back into the emotional stages of anger and sadness

sometimes. But now, I don't stay stuck there as long. Instead, I remind myself that I still have a life to live. That I need to let go of Anthony and my pain because I can't let this breakup destroy me. I know that I can create a bright future for myself—I just have to keep practicing these skills to stop my symptoms, change my reactions, and let go of the past. My future isn't with Anthony, so I need to move on.

Do you see the stages of grief in Laila's story? After the initial shock of her breakup, Laila was stuck in the denial and bargaining phases as she internally wrestled with the reality that her relationship was over. When she learned that Anthony had already moved on with someone else, the emotional stage characterized by deep anger, guilt, and sadness emerged. As she practiced her CBT skills, she began to accept the breakup by reminding herself of the bigger picture of her life. As she did, she spent less time in the early phases of grief and more time focusing on accepting her breakup and moving on.

Like Laila, your breakup probably caused you to go through a grieving process. Often people pass through the stages of grief in order, but people can skip around as they encounter triggers and new situations in life (Kübler-Ross 2014). No matter what phase you're in right now, your goal is to come to a place of acceptance so your ex and this breakup no longer occupy so much space in your life.

EXERCISE: Grieving Your Breakup

As Laila did, reflect on your breakup as a grieving process. In your journal, describe how the stages of grief relate to your experience. After your breakup, were you in shock? Denial? Did you bargain with yourself to try to get back with your ex? Did you feel stuck in anger, guilt, or sadness? Are you starting to accept your breakup more? Can you acknowledge your relationship journey—in all its wonderful and miserable glory—without sliding into a tailspin of exaholic symptoms?

Next, I want you to reflect on what you've learned from this breakup. What positive things came from your relationship? How did you actually benefit from this breakup? For example, after describing her stages of grief, Laila wrote the following in her journal:

As much as I hated going through this breakup, I learned a lot from it. If Anthony hadn't broken up with me, I wouldn't have deeply explored the influence my past has on how I function in romantic relationships. My mom died when I was nine, and my issues with abandonment are much more obvious to me now—they affected my reactions to Anthony both when we were together and after he left. I also learned that he wasn't as great of a partner for me as I once thought. Although I love him, he's really immature, and we didn't actually have much in common. I know that I wouldn't have left him—my childhood core beliefs made me cling to him for dear life. So, in the long run, it's probably better for both of us that he broke up with me. Perhaps the biggest gift of this breakup is learning that I'm much stronger than I thought. If I can get through losing my mom and Anthony, I can get through anything.

The more you're able to radically accept your breakup and embrace it as a learning experience, the easier it'll be to let go of your pain and your ex (Kansky and Allen 2018). Whenever you explore your grieving process and practice acceptance, record it in your log as a self-care intervention.

As you embrace a larger perspective of your life journey, it'll also become easier to see the ways you unintentionally contributed to your own suffering during this breakup. That may sound really strange, but when you're going through an exaholic breakup it's easy to feel like a victim—of your ex's behavior and choices, of your upbringing, of the unfairness of the world. It's much harder to look in the mirror and see how you've contributed to your own heartache. When you learn to look at yourself from a broader, more objective perspective, it's easier to leave the "victimized" role and take on the "participant" role. This very important shift in perspective moves you out of a place of wounded weakness to a place of strength from which you have some control over your life. You always want to make choices from a place of strength because doing so helps you take your power back and feel grounded in your own skin in spite of painful life experiences. Seeing your role in creating relationship distress—while you were with your ex and since breaking up—also helps you develop empathy and compassion for yourself and your ex over time (Enright 2001). Let's explore this further.

Taking Responsibility for Your Role

All relationship struggles are affected by both people involved and have ripple effects on everyone else in our lives (Bobby 2015). Not only did your ex do things that ultimately hurt you, but you undoubtedly did things that hurt them. You also may have hurt others as you experienced this breakup, including family, friends, and even people you think are your enemies, like your ex's new love interest. Often the harm we cause others is unintentional; we have no desire to hurt others, or even an awareness that what we're doing is harmful. When we're in our most pained state, however, sometimes we do things to deliberately punish those we think caused it.

Accepting that we bear some responsibility for the messy aftershocks of a failed relationship makes it easier to let go of past pain because we remember that we're all human. And, consequently, we're all flawed. We all have baggage. Every one of us is fighting an internal battle over some painful past experiences that the outside world can't necessarily see or understand. This includes your ex, your parents, your friends, and even your enemies. As we clumsily try to figure ourselves out and grapple with our wounds, we affect each other. Sometimes we really hurt each other. Romantic love doesn't spare any of us. We're very likely to have our hearts broken in this lifetime, and we're also very likely to break someone else's heart (Baumeister, Wotman, and Stillwell 1993).

Taking responsibility for your role in hurting yourself and others isn't intended to make you feel ashamed or to make you dwell on your mistakes. It also doesn't mean that you weren't victimized in some way; it's quite possible that you were abused or mistreated by your ex, during your upbringing, or in past relationships. That said, shifting your perspective from *What my ex did to me* to *What I did to hurt my ex, others, and myself because of this breakup* will help you feel empowered, because this shift is something you can choose (Enright 2001). You can't change the past, but you can always change how you act, react, and think now.

Some of the ways you may have hurt your ex, others, and yourself during this breakup include:

Hurting Your Ex

- Expressing anger in aggressive ways (like yelling, hitting, name-calling, or intentionally saying mean things to hurt them).

- Violating their boundaries (like hacking into their email or continuing to communicate with them when they've asked you to stop).

- Blaming them for your feelings or actions.

- Lying, cheating, or trying to manipulate them.

- Trying to ruin their reputation or other relationships.

Hurting Others

- Being so preoccupied by your own issues that you aren't available to support loved ones.

- Isolating yourself or not staying close to friends and family.

- Being unavailable to loved ones or forgetful of events that matter to them (like birthdays, holidays, or important dates).

- Neglecting responsibilities (like not performing well at work, doing well at school, or taking care of kids or pets).

- Lashing out at your ex's friends or new dating partners (like posting mean comments on social media or sharing confidential information publicly to hurt them).

Hurting Yourself

- Acting in ways that physically and emotionally hurt you (like self-harm behavior, binge eating, drinking too much, or acting in a sexually promiscuous way).

- Violating your own values and boundaries (like doing things you know aren't consistent with your moral or ethical principles).

- Staying in relationships or situations that aren't healthy when you know you should leave.

- Beating yourself up for mistakes (like telling yourself you are a loser or have no value).

- Neglecting your own physical, emotional, and spiritual well-being.

- Allowing this breakup to define you and losing your core identity as an individual.

Honestly owning the ways that you've contributed to the suffering of others and yourself is critical to healing. In fact, it's one of the foundational tenets of 12-step programs, because when you see yourself as a participant in this experience of love and loss instead of just a victim, your heart will soften (Alcoholics Anonymous World Services, Inc. 2003). You'll start to feel compassion, empathy, and maybe even gratitude for your ex, yourself, and your entire breakup situation (Enright 2001). As you do, you can make amends for your role even if others never apologize for theirs.

EXERCISE: Making Amends

In your journal, describe the ways you intentionally and unintentionally hurt your ex, others, and yourself because of this breakup.

Then, craft a genuine apology letter to each person. This isn't a letter you necessarily want to share; it's really an exercise for yourself. In fact, given that contact with your ex fuels the exaholic cycle, I would encourage you not to share this sentiment with them until or unless you think you're ready. That said, it's often helpful to apologize to people you want to be closer to, because being vulnerable can allow for bonding. Apologizing shows that you care about them, that you're aware you may have hurt them because of your own struggles, and that you're sorry for that. It also creates a dialogue about how you can remedy and repair your relationship with them.

As you think about crafting an apology letter or letters, let's return to Laila's story for an example. Although Laila wasn't going to send the letter to Anthony, she wrote this apology in her journal as if she were talking to him:

Dear Anthony,

As I reflect on our breakup, I know that I did things to hurt you. I sent you mean emails and text messages. I bad-mouthed you to our mutual friends. I called you and your new girlfriend mean names. I did these things because I was so hurt and angry that you left. And I'm sorry. I'm sorry for trying to cause you pain and for acting in ways that may have hurt you. You were a massively important person in my life for a long time, and I don't want to hold on to any negativity toward you. I'm actively taking steps to change so I don't intentionally hurt you or myself moving forward.

Laila

Laila also realized that she may have hurt some of her best friends and family members because of her love addiction to Anthony. Of course, loved ones generally appreciate the natural give-and-take of relationships and want to be there to support you through tough times, but it's still important to take responsibility for the ways you may have harmed them or your relationships with them because of this breakup. Laila wrote the following to her best friend, Suki:

Dear Suki,

You already know that this breakup has been one of the most painful experiences of my life. You've supported me through it and I'm so thankful for that. You're such a dear friend and I love you. As I come out of this dark time, I know that I've been so focused on my own pain that I haven't been as available to support and connect with you as I want to be. I want you to know that I'm sorry for that. You mean so much to me. If there's anything I can do to be there for you, I'd love to hear from you.

Love,

Laila

Finally, Laila wrote herself a letter. This might feel strange to you because we don't usually apologize or talk to ourselves. That said, Laila's symptoms of love addiction led her to think and act in ways that ultimately hurt her deeply. So, she wrote herself this simple apology:

Dear Self,

My symptoms following this breakup led me to think, feel, and act in ways I don't like. And I'm sorry. I'm sorry for the ways that I lost myself. For chasing after someone who doesn't want me anymore. For doubting my own value. For not taking care of my health. For drinking too much. For neglecting my friends. For becoming bitter and resentful, lashing out at Anthony and his new girlfriend. I want to be better than that. And I want to be happy again. So, I'm actively taking steps to change. I'm learning and practicing new CBT skills every day. I refuse to let this breakup lead me down a path of self-destruction anymore. I'm committed to treating myself and everyone I love better moving forward.

Love,

Me

Taking responsibility for your role by making amends is ultimately empowering, because you can see what you did to make your situation worse, own it, and change it. It also allows you to talk more intimately with loved ones about your breakup journey and repair any rifts that may have opened along the way. As you make amends, you'll be inching closer to probably the toughest task on your healing journey: forgiving the past.

The Power of Forgiveness

Forgiving your past is probably one of the hardest things you'll ever try to do, because when bad things happen that we don't want or deeply hurt us—like this breakup—our ego-based minds focus on all the reasons we deserve to be angry and blame others for our pain (Enright 2001). We're excellent at keeping track of people who harmed us—your ex, parents, friends, family, childhood influences, God, or even yourself. In moments of intense pain, you won't want to forgive because you'll want revenge first, or to be given a reason that convinces you someone deserves to be forgiven (Myss 2008).

The truth is that forgiveness is a choice (Enright 2001). It's the act of letting go of resentment and anger toward another person who you believe mistreated you. Forgiveness isn't given because it's deserved—it's given so the pain of the past doesn't eat you alive in the present. Forgiving someone doesn't mean that what happened was okay. It doesn't mean you approve of someone's behavior that was morally or ethically wrong. It doesn't mean that their choices didn't hurt you. It doesn't even mean you want the person you're trying to forgive to be in your life ever again! What forgiveness means is that you refuse to let the pain of the past ruin your present. That you won't allow yourself to dwell in misery. That you won't take your wounds out on others. As you learn to forgive, you free yourself from an internal emotional prison, and sometimes you free the other person as well.

When we experience deep emotional pain and grieve a serious loss—as you have been while going through this breakup—you really have two basic choices for how you'll respond. On the one hand, you can let your pain break your spirit, passing your misery on to everyone around you and allowing it to ruin your enjoyment of life now and in the future. This choice can keep you self-righteously bitter, leading you to become depressed and chronically angry. On the other hand, you can actively practice accepting your breakup, seeing it as an opportunity for growth, and forgiving any painful experiences from the past so that they don't ruin your present (Enright 2001). In other words, you can stay fixated on past pain, mired in the exaholic cycle for years, or you can actively practice forgiving old wounds so that they don't destroy your future. Clearly, you'll benefit greatly by choosing the latter.

If you believe in a higher power, having faith that something greater than you is benevolently watching over you and in charge of the universal laws of justice can be important to your forgiveness process (Alcoholics Anonymous World Services, Inc. 2003; Myss 2008). From this perspective, we're not capable of understanding why everything happens in life, but we can trust that there's a higher reason for it (Enright 2001; Miller 1999). Even though we're not in control, we're capable of controlling how we respond to every situation we encounter. The ultimate goal with forgiveness is to respond in ways—with compassion, empathy, endurance, understanding, humility, kindness, and forgiveness—that reflect the very best of humanity and not the worst (Enright 2001; Myss 2008).

EXERCISE: Choosing to Forgive

You're going to practice the very difficult process of forgiving your ex. Start by describing the things about your ex that you're struggling to forgive—all the ways they hurt you. This list can include your ex's behavior, their choices, things they said, broken promises, physical harm, financial costs, or any specific experiences you keep reliving in your mind that keep you stuck in the past. It can also include the effect this breakup has had on your psychological, physical, and spiritual well-being: being stuck in the exaholic cycle, hurting others, not sleeping, losing hope in humanity, becoming depressed, doubting God—write it all down. See your wounds in black and white.

As you look at what you wrote, think about how keeping these wounds active in your mind and heart affects you. What'll happen to you if you don't forgive your ex and continue to hold on to resentment about the past? What'll happen if you do forgive them? After looking at the pros and cons of forgiveness, actively choose to forgive them. See that your ex—and anyone else who's hurt you—is a human being just like you. They have their own wounds, their own hurts, their own spiritual growth to do in this life. Forgiveness is not about excusing their behavior; it's about acknowledging that you can let go of the pain you're experiencing if you actively choose to.

Let's look at Laila's "forgiveness" journal entry as an example:

I absolutely hate that Anthony broke up with me and that he started dating another girl right away—maybe even before we broke up. He told me we'd always be together, that he loved me and wanted me by his side. It turns out that isn't true anymore. I want to punish him for getting me to believe in us because I've been so hurt and lost in the aftermath of our breakup.

If I don't forgive him, my resentment and sadness will continue to eat me up inside. He did some things that really hurt me. But if I stay bitter about them—even if I have good reason to be angry—where does that leave me? Bitter and stuck in past pain. If I do forgive him, I'm choosing to let go of my pain so I can build a new life without him. So, I'm choosing to try to forgive him. The truth is that I probably also hurt him. He didn't have an easy upbringing either, and it affects how he acts in romantic relationships, just as mine does. I think he loved me at one point, but he changed. And that's okay. Do I really want him to stay with me just because he said he would if he doesn't want to be with me anymore? Clearly not. So, I want to forgive him. I'm letting go of the past, and I hope he forgives me someday, too, for the harm I caused him.

Holding on to resentment and anger toward your ex hurts you because it keeps you in a victimized state of past pain. Even if you have a very good reason to be resentful and bitter, you only hurt yourself by staying mired in these emotions. In addition to your ex, you may also want to forgive others who've hurt you, like your parents, past lovers, and even yourself. Continue to practice forgiving anyone who's mistreated you, and record it in your log as a self-care intervention.

Moving Forward

As you grieve and come to accept that your relationship is over, you can let go of past pain by taking responsibility for your role, apologizing to those you've hurt along the way, and actively choosing to forgive. The more empathy and compassion you can develop for yourself and others, the better, because we've all lived through something that rocked us to our core. You can't avoid pain and loss in life; they're an inevitable part of the journey. Instead, the goal is to learn from every experience and make choices that reflect better versions of ourselves along the way.

All the work you're doing now is freeing up energy to put toward creating a wonderful future. The space your ex used to occupy is now a blank page waiting for you to write on. In the next chapter, we're going to identify and explore your values, the fundamental principles that you believe are central to living a good life. You can use those values to make choices that guide your future.

CHAPTER 8

Letting Your Values Guide Your Choices

It's been ten months since I last talked to my ex. Seeing this breakup as a grieving process helps me forgive her and myself for the ways we hurt each other. To mend relationships with friends and family that suffered along the way. And to apologize for my role. As I do, it's easier to let go of my hurt because I see that she's on her own life journey, just like me. If she doesn't want me anymore, that's her choice. Maybe it's the best thing for her! So, I need to let her go and focus on healing myself.

This breakup affected me deeply, but I'm actively trying to move on. The hard part now is that I'm not sure what I actually want. What does my life look like without my ex in it? There's a gaping hole where he used to be and I don't know what to fill it with. It's like I need to find myself again, but I'm not sure how.

It's been three years since my divorce and I'm finally moving out of the exaholic cycle. My friends are encouraging me to date again. I think I'm finally ready to find another life partner, but I don't seem to pick people who are very healthy for me. I now see that I have some very flawed foundational core beliefs from childhood that affect who I'm attracted to in really unhealthy ways. So, how do I pick people who'll be good for me? I'm afraid because I never want to go through this again.

As you come to accept your breakup, the heavy emotional anchors that kept you drowning in the sea of faulty foundational core beliefs begin lifting.

Whereas heartache once consumed you, space emerges for creating something new. You're coming to a place of great freedom. This part of your recovery can be really exciting because your life is opening up, making way for fresh new opportunities and experiences. But as is true for some of the exaholics in the stories above, this freedom can be daunting if you're not sure what you really want.

Going through an exaholic breakup leaves most of us feeling lost for a while. You may be reevaluating who you are, what you really stand for, and what gives your life significance now that your relationship's over. As humans, we thrive when we believe we have a purpose on this planet (Frankl 1962). When we have a reason to get up in the morning, motivated to move in the direction of something that really matters in the grand scheme of life. So, it's incredibly helpful in this time of transition to explore your values and use them to guide your choices. As you do, you'll rebuild your self-esteem because you'll be living in a way that's consistent with what *you* think makes life meaningful (Kesberg and Keller 2018). The better you feel about yourself, the more willing you'll be to take risks that catapult you into your next adventure—to make new friends, try different hobbies, and even date again—because you'll know that you have the internal strength to handle whatever comes your way. And it all starts with exploring what's most important to you.

Exploring Your Values

Personal values are the stable, underlying beliefs you hold about what's most important to living a good and meaningful life (Oyserman 2015; Schwartz 1992). They're the principles that you believe define the best of humanity—what you want to emulate and what you admire in others—as well as the traits you find most offensive and off-putting (Chrystal, Karl, and Fischer 2019; Kesberg and Keller 2018). Your values guide your likes and dislikes, what you think makes someone good or bad, and how you think people should live (Rokeach 1973; Schwartz 1992).

When you think about your values, what immediately comes to mind? Maybe you value *ambition*, admiring people who go after what they want without allowing the paralyzing fear of failure or self-doubt to stop them. Maybe you value *humility* and appreciate people who are modest even after experiencing triumphant successes, and you bristle at those who continually brag or name-drop. Maybe you value *perseverance*, marveling at people who work to overcome hardships, like the devastating effects of war or abuse. Or maybe it's *family* relationships, treating others with *respect*, living life according to a *spiritual* or religious tradition, showing *restraint* and self-control instead of indulging, or acting *honorably* to fight for individual human rights and freedoms.

You started developing your values in childhood as your family, culture, peers, friends, and early dating experiences taught you about the social rules governing your environment. As we explored in chapter 6, you learned what made someone an important and valued member of your community by observing and interacting with your surroundings. Over time, you adopted many of the values of your culture as personally relevant and universally true (Rokeach 1973; Schwartz 1992). Although there are some virtue-based values that most humans endorse as central to the human experience—like *honesty*, *freedom*, and *justice*—what you care about most will be unique to you (Oyserman 2015; Schwartz 1992). And although this breakup undoubtedly changed you in some meaningful ways, your most cherished values have probably remained the same because they tend to be relatively stable over the course of our lives (Schwartz 1992).

Living in accordance with your values is part of how you create meaning and purpose in your life (Ponizovskiy et al. 2019; Schwartz 1992). When your actions reflect what you believe matters most—despite what anyone else may think—you become more authentic and trustworthy (Kesberg and Keller 2018). When you're feeling lost or sensitive, you'll sometimes violate your own values or want someone else to tell you how to live. Yet, the more you defy your own moral compass or live according to what others tell you makes you valuable, the more disappointed you'll become, because meaning isn't given to you or determined by others. You give your life meaning by making choices that reflect what you believe really matters (Frankl 1962; Yalom 1980). When your values don't guide your actions, you'll start to question your moral character, your integrity, and even your ability to trust yourself because your words won't have any applied significance (Chrystal, Karl, and Fischer 2019; Kesberg and Keller 2018). When what you say doesn't match how you act, you'll feel like a fraud who isn't authentically living your life, and that'll leave you feeling weak and lost.

Ideally, your personal values are reflected in all areas of your life, including your romantic relationships. So, let's explore what matters the most to you.

EXERCISE: Assessing Your Personal Values

Look at the following list of value-based words and identify those that resonate with you the most—the ones that describe what you really stand for, that represent values that you feel shouldn't be violated. Circle them here or write them in your journal. If there's a value that you hold dear that's not on the list, record it at the end of the list or in your journal as well. (To see more value-based words, feel free to download the Personal Values in Romantic Relationships Questionnaire at this book's website: http://www.newharbinger.com/50379. It includes an expanded word list.) There are no right or wrong answers, so really consider what you think is most important to living a good life.

Achievement	Friendship	Loyalty
Commitment	Freedom	Openness
Communication	Honesty	Peace
Cooperation	Independence	Personal growth
Fairness	Intuition	Pride
Family	Kindness	Privacy

Rationality	Safety/security	Understanding
Respect	Service	_____
Reliability	Spirituality/	_____
Responsibility	religion	_____
Resilience	Success	

Next, pick the five values that stand out as being most important to you and note them in your journal. Keep your list close at hand, because we're going to use it to guide your choices later in this chapter.

As you remember and rediscover the values you hold most dear, you can make choices that reflect them (Kesberg and Keller 2018; Oyserman 2015). This is critically important to your psychological well-being because it boosts your self-esteem and self-efficacy—your sense of control over the direction of your life. No matter what obstacles you encounter moving forward, you'll feel stronger and more empowered when you make choices that align with your moral principles, even when others don't (Chrystal, Karl, and Fischer 2019). Let's explore this idea further.

Making Choices That Reflect Your Values

As you move into the next phase of your life without your ex, you want your values to guide your choices. As simple as that may sound, it's actually very tricky, because values in and of themselves don't actually describe or prescribe specific behaviors that honor them (Ponizovskiy et al. 2019). For example, if *loyalty* is one of your core values, your idea of what loyal or disloyal behavior looks like may differ from that of your friends, family members, or romantic partners. To complicate matters further, behavior that reflects your values may look different in the diverse areas of your life (Oyserman 2015). For example, being a loyal friend may look very different from being a loyal romantic partner or parent. So, although your values ideally guide all your choices and actions, how your behavior reflects your values can be highly subjective and situation-specific (Kesberg and Keller 2018; Oyserman 2015).

Let's consider a few examples of how behavior may reflect values:

- If *personal growth* is one of your most esteemed values, you may continually strive to understand yourself more deeply by reading self-help books, going to therapy, and attending wellness retreats. You may look down on people who seem superficial or stuck in their ways because you see their behavior as a violation of this value.

- If you value *safety*, you may only want to be in seriously committed romantic relationships with people who are financially secure and emotionally grounded. You may choose partners who are predictable and dislike casual dating because it feels unsafe.

- If *achievement* is one of your core values, you may choose to work a full-time job at a company you deem reputable because success and status in life are important to you. Conversely, you may become annoyed with people who seem lazy or lack the intrinsic motivation to work hard and excel.

- If you value *family*, you may prioritize time with your kids, parents, and spouse over others. You may look down on people who get divorced and choose to stay in relationships with difficult or dysfunctional relatives because cutting them out of your life disrupts your moral compass.

- If *independence* is a core value of yours, you might avoid serious relationships because you dislike long-term commitments. If someone's too needy, you move on quickly. You might not even want to own a home or your own furniture because having a mortgage and physical items that don't fit into a suitcase or backpack makes you feel suffocated and tied down.

- If you value *friendship*, you may spend a great deal of time cultivating your connection with others. You're willing to work through conflict and do things your friends like to do—even when you don't really enjoy them—because you want to show others how important friendship is to you.

- If *responsibility* is a value of yours, you strive to see your faults and work on changing them while apologizing for your mistakes. You may be easily irritated when people blame others for their actions, lie, or lack personal accountability. When your kids don't clean up their room or do their homework on time, it bothers you because you consider this behavior irresponsible—a violation of this value.

In the examples above, do you see the connection between specific values and the corresponding choices you could make to reflect them? Let's explore that connection in your life next.

EXERCISE: Reflecting on Your Value-Based Choices

Using the five most important values you identified in the last exercise, think about how each is reflected in your life today. Remember that, ideally, your values influence your choices and behavior in all areas of your life. So, in your journal, describe how each value affects your romantic relationships, parenting, friendships, family interactions, career choices, academic pursuits, spiritual practice, community involvement, or other important areas of your life. For example, if *kindness* is one of your core values, do you strive to be kind to others in all situations you encounter? Do you aspire to communicate in a kind way with work colleagues, family members, friends, your ex, and yourself? Do you apologize when you're not kind? Do you shift unkind thoughts that run through your mind because they violate your moral code?

Next, in your journal I want you to describe the ways you violated your values during your relationship and how they aren't reflected in your life right now. As I've already noted, going through an exaholic breakup often leads us to act in ways that aren't consistent with our personal values, which ultimately leaves us feeling ashamed and regretful (Chrystal, Karl, and Fischer 2019). Here are some ways you may have violated your own values during this breakup:

- If you value *honesty*, lying to or trying to manipulate your ex or other loved ones.

- If you value *respect*, negatively labeling yourself and others or treating people as if they don't have inherent value when you don't like them.

- If you value *loyalty*, cheating on your ex or engaging in sexual or romantic behavior with someone who was married or in a committed relationship.

- If you value *communication*, not honestly sharing your thoughts and feelings with your ex in a respectful way. Or yelling, blaming, and intentionally trying to harm people through your words.

- If you value *intuition*, not trusting your gut when you felt that something wasn't right.

- If you value *spirituality*, losing your connection to a higher power or acting in ways that don't reflect a divine path.

As you think about how you compromised your values over the course of your relationship and subsequent breakup, it's time to take action (Ponizovskiy et al. 2019). What do you want to add to your life that reflects your values? What are some things you'll never do again because they're inconsistent with your values? As you consider your value-based choices, I don't want you only to think about the "big decisions" you make, like what job you take, where you live, or whether you have kids. Of course, these are massively important choices; hopefully your values will influence or have influenced these choices because they dramatically affect your life! But it's the hundreds of seemingly small choices you make each day in the company of your own mind that affect your well-being the most. For example, if one of your core values is *compassion*, you can violate this principle when you think a judgmental thought about your ex, tell yourself you're pathetic for struggling, or roll your eyes at your sister-in-law when she annoyingly tells you the same painful story over and over. These seemingly small behaviors reflect your values, too. If they fly in the face of what you claim to believe, they'll also hurt your self-esteem and self-respect.

In addition, I want you to be aware that behavior you interpret as a violation of your values may not be viewed that way by others. For instance, if you value *respect*, you'll probably judge your romantic partners harshly when they act in ways you think are disrespectful—anything from continually coming home late to dismissing your feelings to flirting with someone else. Yet, your partner may not intend to be disrespectful or even agree with your perspective that their behavior is problematic! It's important to be able to untangle your values (in this case, *respect*) from the corresponding behavior that you think reflects or doesn't reflect it, so you can communicate more effectively with others.

Finally, it's likely your ex did things that violated your values during your relationship and breakup. If this exercise reminds you of that, describe the values you think your ex violated and how. Then, use a CBT exercise like radical acceptance or forgiveness to let go of your energetic connection to past pain. Remind yourself that your ex's behavior reflects their values and who they are, not who you are, and that you want to move on. In addition, when you notice that you're violating your values in some way, pause, record it in your log, and practice a self-care intervention until you can make a healthier choice.

As you think about incorporating your values into your choices more deliberately, you may be wondering how this applies to future romantic relationships. You may be very wary of dating right now because you never want to go through an exaholic breakup again. Plus, when you do start dating, you're really acknowledging the end of your relationship by pursuing new potential mates, and you're making yourself vulnerable to new love interests again. All of that can be pretty scary, so let me reassure you that it's very healthy for you to be single! Take as much time as you need to heal before jumping into the dating world, and try not to feel pressure to hasten the process.

That said, we often learn the most about ourselves in relationships—especially romantic relationships—because interacting with others is like looking in a mirror: your reactions always tell you something about yourself. Even if you're not going to date for a while, planning ways to bring your values into your romantic life will help you in the future. So, let's explore how you might do that.

Applying Your Values to Romantic Love

You already intuitively know that there are many kinds of love (Tobore 2020). The love you feel for a romantic partner is very different from the love you feel for your children, a parent, a friend, a social cause, your country, or a pet. In fact, emerging research suggests that within romantic relationships there are at least three different kinds of love that stimulate different parts of the brain: *lust*, *romantic love*, and *attachment* (Fisher 2016; Fisher et al. 2002). Understanding them can help you make value-based choices when you start dating again.

Romantic relationships often start with *lust*, which is really your sex drive (Fisher 2016; Fisher et al. 2002). When dating, most of us start by searching for someone we find sexually attractive—a person who looks, smells, dresses, and acts in ways we find seductive. That may sound somewhat superficial, but unless you've only been in arranged relationships that aren't love-based at the start (Regan, Lakhanpal, and Anguiano 2012), you're generally going to date people you find physically attractive. If you're not sexually interested at least somewhat, you probably won't make it past the first date—or even *to* the first date! So, think of lust as the search for a sexual partner. It's what drives you to check people out in social situations, like at a nightclub, a class at school, or even the grocery store. If you're lucky, someone catches your eye: there's a gaze, chemistry, something you find attractive about them. Biologically, lust is your body's way of encouraging you to look for and find a mate to have sex with so that you'll have children and ensure the survival of our species (Fisher 2016). Your brain rewards you for looking for sexual partners (and having sex with them) by pumping you full of blissful hormones and neurotransmitters.

The problem with dating people you feel lust for is that it doesn't have anything to do with your values. Lust is physically and sexually wired into your evolutionary survival system (Fisher et al. 2002). You can feel lust for almost anyone you think is good-looking or attractive somehow—even people you don't really know, like, or even want to be around! And you can feel lust for many people at once because it has very little to do with a person's character and much more to do with what they look like or the way you feel when you're around them (Fisher 2016). So, although your sex drive attracts you to people, feeling lust for someone doesn't necessarily make them a good romantic partner for you.

Conversely, *romantic love* (Fisher 2004, 2016), or falling in love, is an overwhelming drive to be around one specific person who makes you feel amazing. This form of love is central to what we've been exploring in this book because it's the cornerstone of most love addiction. When you fall in love, you become possessive of and hyperfocused on your lover, craving their time and attention because no one else makes you feel the way they do (Earp et al. 2017). Even the terms we use to describe romantic love allude to its power: you become "lovesick" and fall "head over heels" because you're so "madly in love" that your lover "takes your breath away." Feeling romantic love for someone makes them the center of your internal world. Like lust, however, romantic love doesn't ensure that you and your love interest have similar values because it's also an evolutionary drive aimed at encouraging you to have children and raise them with a partner long enough to survive (Fisher 2016). If your relationship started with lust and moved into romantic love—you were sexually attracted to someone and eventually fell for them— you may, at some point, come to the shocking realization that you're in love with someone you don't actually like or have anything in common with! In long-term relationships, that's unlikely to turn out well.

Finally, if your relationship lasts long enough, you may come to a place of romantic *attachment* with your mate (Fisher 2016). Being attached isn't as hot and steamy as feeling lust or falling in love, but it's the deepest, most conscious kind of love. Being attached offers comfort, security, and devotion in a bonded way (Bobby 2015; Mellody, Miller, and Miller 2003). Attachment also often reflects a more honest acceptance of who you are, who your partner is, and the choice to be a couple. To become and remain attached—to live on parallel paths with another person—takes dedication, commitment, care, understanding, and effort. Although being attached doesn't ensure that your values are compatible, you're much more likely to want to stay attached to someone who shares your beliefs about how you want to live and what makes life meaningful.

The ideal relationship situation for most people who want a fulfilling long-term connection is to fall in love with someone they're sexually attracted to who also shares similar values. This is very hard to achieve in real life because we usually start dating from a place of lust, which has almost nothing to do with who your partner is on the inside! If you hook up with someone you're lusting over and then fall into romantic love, you're now driven to be intimately connected to someone who may not share your values, lifestyle preferences, or goals. So, as you start dating again, I encourage you to find people you *like* because they share your values. If you date people who hold similar beliefs about what makes life meaningful, you'll probably admire, enjoy, and respect them if you do eventually fall in love because you'll appreciate who they are on the inside! In addition, even if you don't lust over a new mate at first because they aren't physically your type, they'll probably become more attractive to you over time if you really like them and share common values! You'll also enjoy the dating experience much more even if it doesn't turn into a romantic connection. So, let's prepare you to apply your values to future dating.

EXERCISE: Preparing to Date Again

Think about the personal values you identified earlier. What values would you really like to see in a mate? What behavior and lifestyle choices of a future romantic partner would reflect these values? For example, you may like and enjoy dating people who:

- Share an interest or hobby that reflects a core value of yours

- Hold similar political opinions and makes choices based on those beliefs

- Have a passion for something you love (like art, music, travel, or pets) and take time in their life to support it

- Dedicate their time to a cause you care deeply about (like cancer research, women's rights, or environmental protection)

- Have similar relationship and life goals

Next, think about whether you have any *deal breakers*—characteristics or behaviors that contradict your values—that would make you not want to date someone (Jonason et al. 2015). For example, you may not want to fall for someone who:

- Is married or committed to someone else

- Smokes or drinks a lot—or not at all

- Has religious or spiritual beliefs that conflict with yours

- Has political affiliations or beliefs that conflict with yours

- Has different desires for children and family

- Wants a type of relationship that's different from what you want (for example, a long-term monogamous relationship, an open relationship, or something casual)

- Has a personal characteristic you really dislike (for example, has a way of speaking or eating that you hate, is too short or too tall)

- Has poor self-care and hygiene

When you do start dating, it's helpful to be able to detect warning signs that a new dating partner may not be emotionally available or healthy for you because of their own issues. Although the topic of navigating romantic relationships is far too big to cover in this book, I would pause and reevaluate a dating partner if they regularly do the following:

- Don't express anger respectfully or act abusively

- Send inconsistent or mixed messages (for example, they call a lot and then not at all or treat you as if you're very important sometimes but are aloof other times)

- Fear commitment or keep you at arm's length (for example, they leave future plans unclear or vague or don't want to introduce you to their friends and family)

- Devalue you (for example, they joke about how silly you are in a half-true, half-mocking way or compare your looks in a negative way to someone they find highly attractive)

- Have difficulty respectfully communicating their perspective (for example, instead of sharing their thoughts, feelings, and perspective, they talk about what's wrong with you or how you need to change so they'll feel better)

- Play games with you (for example, manipulate you to make you interested in them, pretend to be unavailable to look important, or try to make you feel jealous or hurt)

- Are suspicious of you without reason

- Communicate in a passive-aggressive way (for example, they don't state their feelings directly but make side comments that indicate they don't like something you're doing)

- Try to control you or are too possessive

Anyone who consistently treats their partner in these ways has some work to do on themselves before they can have a healthy romantic relationship. Similarly, if you notice yourself acting in these ways, pause and start working at a deeper level, because those behaviors won't serve you or any of your relationships well. (See "Recommended Readings and Resources" at the end of this book if you'd like to explore this topic further.)

When you start dating again, I recommend taking sexual activity slowly because it floods your system with dopamine and brings to the surface unresolved feelings about your ex, which can trigger exaholic symptoms (Bobby 2015; Fisher 2016). Engaging in sexual activity—even with someone you think you'd never fall for, don't like as a person, or don't share any values with—can make you more likely to fall in love with them.

Moving Forward

As you identify your values and make choices that reflect them, you'll become more self-confident and authentic. This empowers you to try new things—make new friends, try different hobbies, and even date again—because you'll trust that you can handle whatever opportunities and obstacles are thrown your way. Not all of your choices are going to work well; you may try something new and hate it, which is perfectly okay! Most of our learning comes through experiences, and sometimes they turn out to be unfortunate! The key to growth isn't trying to be perfect by not making mistakes; it's not repeating the same mistakes over and over!

In the last chapter, we're going to review what you've learned and how you've changed since you started this book. We're also going to reassess your symptoms and make a plan to maintain your gains moving forward.

CHAPTER 9

Moving Forward Authentically

It's been a year since I last talked to my ex. As much as this breakup was excruciating to go through, I can honestly say that it was a blessing in disguise. Losing my ex forced me to reevaluate my entire life. I have a more honest view of myself in relationships—what's hard for me about intimacy and why. I'm more empathic and compassionate toward others. I'm learning to forgive and let go of my anger. I'm making choices that reflect my values, and I'm starting to trust myself again. I never thought any good could come out of this breakup, but it has.

I haven't been an active part of my ex's life in over ten years, but I've thought about her every day. I didn't really deal with our divorce when it happened. I tried to move on too quickly to distract myself from the pain. As I practice these skills, my perspective has completely changed even though the facts are exactly the same. For the first time, I'm grateful for our relationship—and for our breakup. I finally see a positive future for myself without her in it. I'm hopeful for the first time in years and it feels so good!

The biggest gift of this breakup is that I know that I'm okay alone. That's such a powerful realization that I only learned because I loved and lost my ex.

You've been on an incredible introspective journey. When you opened this book for the first time you were probably really suffering. All of us who've lived through a love-addicted breakup know the consuming symptoms that keep us stuck knee-deep in our pain. When you're mired in the misery of it all, it's nearly impossible to view your story of love and loss from the broader perspective that the map of your life offers. As your symptoms weaken their mighty grip, it becomes easier to do this. Little by little, the fact that this is just one of many important relationships you'll have in this lifetime starts to come into focus.

The truth is that you aren't the same person you were before you met your ex. And that's not a bad thing! The journey of life offers experiences that shape you, help you learn, and give you the opportunity to evolve into a more honest, authentic version of yourself (J. S. Beck 2021; Ellis and Harper 1997). You won't emerge from this breakup only to go back to the same life you had before meeting your ex. Instead, you'll integrate into your identity the wisdom of what you learned from this experience. Accepting the loss of your relationship allows for a wiser you to emerge, inspired to discover what really matters to you now. And as you use your values to guide your choices, a lighter, transformed self comes forth from the muddy waters of this experience to start your next adventure.

In this chapter, we'll reflect on what you've learned and how you've changed since you started recovering from this breakup. As we celebrate the effort and progress you've made, we'll target any lingering symptoms that're still giving you trouble and plan for setbacks you may encounter along the way. Let's start by reviewing your learning and by measuring your progress.

Reflecting on Your Journey

You now know a lot about love addiction and how it affected your breakup experience. Starting in part 1 of this book, you learned that falling in love looks a lot like being addicted to a drug, and it can leave you with some miserable symptoms after a breakup (Fisher, Aron, and Brown 2005; Fisher 2016; Fisher et al. 2002; Sanches and John 2019). You learned the primary symptoms of a love-addicted breakup—the obsessive and intrusive thinking, strong cravings, emotional distress and reactivity, and harmful compulsive and impulsive acting-out behaviors (Costa et al. 2019; Earp et al. 2017; Fisher 2016; Peele and Brodsky 1975)—and examined them in relation to your life. You saw that these symptoms function in an exaholic cycle that's driven by a desire to "use," or be in contact with your ex because feeling close to them makes you feel temporarily better. After the contact ends, however, your symptoms balloon and escalate, tormenting you until you make contact again. This cycle keeps you trapped in a miserable loop of symptoms that eats away at your health, self-esteem, and ability to enjoy your life.

After assessing your symptoms and their costs to your well-being, you started taking action by practicing many CBT skills designed to help you intervene in the exaholic cycle itself (J. S. Beck 2021; Tolin 2016). You tracked your symptoms using self-monitoring logs to see how they functioned in your life. You minimized contact with your ex to stop fueling the cycle. You used thought-stopping and rumination time to fight unwanted and unpleasant obsessive thinking. You rode out your urges to contact your ex instead of giving in to your cravings. You tried to radically accept that your relationship is over and considered the consequences of your behavior before acting. You also learned to identify and manage your triggers—things in life that remind you of your ex and make your symptoms worse—while setting healthy boundaries, increasing your social support, and finding new ways to meet your physical, mental, emotional, and spiritual health needs. As you practiced these skills, you recorded them as self-care interventions in your log to track how your efforts helped you over time.

As you began to feel some relief and control over your symptoms, part 2 of this book took you on a deep dive, exploring how your thoughts and beliefs feed your love addiction. You learned to identify and assess untrue and unhelpful red-flag thinking that fuels your desire to be close to your ex, like being in denial about your breakup, rationalizing harmful behaviors, and jumping to negative conclusions about your future (A. T. Beck et al. 1979; J. S. Beck 2021; Ellis and Harper 1997). You explored some of the faulty conclusions you may have made about your ex that kept you pining after them, like believing they're the best, that you need them to be complete, or that you can make them change. You also uncovered how difficult experiences in your childhood led you to form negative core beliefs about yourself and others that can harm your romantic relationships as an adult (Ainsworth 1989; Bretherton 1992). More specifically, any childhood experiences you may have had that left you feeling unsafe and unloved made it hard for you to trust and be close to romantic partners as an adult (Hazan and Shafer 1987; Levine and Heller 2012). As you became aware of these faulty red-flag thoughts and beliefs, you used the 3 Ds to challenge them: you *detected* your thoughts, *debated* them for accuracy, and *discriminated* the true from the untrue to create a more helpful, self-enhancing perspective based on fundamental Truths about you and this breakup (Ellis and Harper 1997).

After you learned to challenge your faulty thinking, part 3 of this book focused on helping you create the next great chapter of your life. You looked at losing your ex as a grieving process and explored how accepting it frees you to start anew (Kübler-Ross 2014). You shifted from seeing yourself as a victim of this breakup to seeing yourself as a participant in it. From that framework, you examined your role in maintaining your suffering while practicing forgiveness to let go of past pain (Enright 2001). You explored your personal values—what you believe is most important to living a meaningful life—and strengthened your self-esteem as you made choices that reflected them (Oyserman 2015; Schwartz 1992). As your self-confidence grew, trying new things became less scary because you trust that you're capable of handling any challenges life throws your way. You may even decide to start dating again soon—or maybe you already have.

Looking back at the enormous amount of information and number of skills you've learned, my sincerest hope is that you're feeling better. That your symptoms have decreased, your perspective has shifted, and you're confidently moving forward into a new chapter of your life. That really was the goal of this work—to overcome your addiction to your ex and create a new life for yourself that you really want to live. Let's take a moment to see how much you've changed because of your efforts by retaking the Exaholic Assessment Questionnaire.

EXERCISE: Love-Addiction Breakup Assessment

As you did in chapter 1, carefully read each item on the Exaholic Assessment Questionnaire and respond based on your experience *in the last week*. Rate the accuracy of each statement as honestly as you can using the following scale:

1 = not at all true of me   *4 = mostly true of me*

2 = slightly true of me   *5 = completely true of me*

3 = often true of me

Intrusive and Obsessive Thinking

_____ I think about my ex almost all the time.

_____ Unwanted thoughts of my ex pop into my mind unexpectedly and stay stuck there.

_____ In my mind I relive past experiences I had with my ex or rehearse what I'd like to say to them now.

_____ I want to stop thinking about my ex but can't.

Cravings for Contact

_____ I desperately want to contact my ex (for example, to talk to or see them).

_____ I feel strong urges to connect with my ex even though I know it's going to be a negative interaction (like a fight).

_____ It's almost impossible for me not to contact or seek out information about my ex.

_____ When I'm not in contact with my ex I feel terrible.

Emotional Distress and Reactivity

_____ I'm extremely emotionally distressed because of my breakup.

_____ I struggle to feel happiness or pleasure since my ex and I broke up.

_____ I'm more moody and emotionally reactive since my breakup.

_____ I'm emotionally unable to let go of my ex.

Harmful Compulsive and Impulsive Behaviors

_____ I actively try to contact my ex or do things to feel close to them again (for example, calling them, texting them, or looking through old photos).

_____ I actively try to get information about my ex behind their back (for example, through social media or mutual friends).

_____ I act in ways that ultimately hurt me to feel closer to my ex (for example, driving by their home or having sex with them).

_____ I engage in unhealthy behaviors to distract myself from the pain of this breakup (for example, drinking too much, smoking, or binge eating).

Costs to My Well-Being

_____ I struggle to function in my daily life because I can't get over my ex (for example, I'm not performing as well at work or taking care of my physical health).

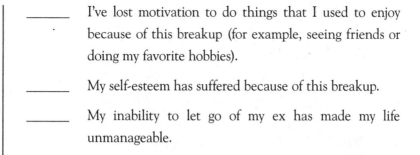

_____ I've lost motivation to do things that I used to enjoy because of this breakup (for example, seeing friends or doing my favorite hobbies).

_____ My self-esteem has suffered because of this breakup.

_____ My inability to let go of my ex has made my life unmanageable.

When you're done, calculate your score by adding together your scores for all twenty items, and then compare the score to that of the first assessment you did in chapter 1. Has your total score decreased, suggesting your symptoms are getting better? Have the items that were most upsetting to you initially—that you scored a 4 or a 5 the first time around—improved? Notice any healthy progress you've made since the first questionnaire and take a moment to appreciate your efforts. You deserve credit for your improvement because you did the daily hard work to change! If you notice that some lingering symptoms are still giving you trouble, that's perfectly okay; make a note of them, because we're going to address those later in this chapter.

Another way to gauge how much you've changed is to look at how your perspective has shifted since you started this healing journey (Lepore and Greenberg 2002; Primeau, Servaty-Seib, and Enersen 2013). The very first exercise you did was to write your relationship story detailing events from the time you met your ex until you started reading this book. Now it's time to describe your process of recovery from this breakup.

EXERCISE: Telling Your Story of Recovery

In your journal, write your story of recovery. Begin with the day you started reading this book, or when you actively tried to stop your addictive symptoms, and describe your journey until today. Include anything about your experience that's important to you—what's been hardest or easiest, skills you've found helpful, memorable moments, important realizations along the way—but be sure to describe how you've changed over time.

To help get you started, let's return to Maria's story from chapter 1. As you may remember, Maria was struggling with an exaholic breakup after the end of her relationship with the love of her life, John. Maria told her story of recovery like this:

When I started recovering from this breakup, I was an absolute mess. My scores on the first Exaholic Assessment Questionnaire were really high, and I had all the symptoms of a love–addicted breakup: I couldn't stop thinking about John, I craved him, and I wanted him back so desperately that I often violated my own boundaries to feel closer to him. My physical and psychological well–being were suffering severely. I was in so much emotional pain that I felt utterly pathetic and lost.

Practicing the CBT skills in this book was so much work, but it really helped me change. I felt like I was doing self–monitoring logs all the time, which I found exhausting! But they also showed me very clearly the patterns I needed to stop to feel better. Cutting off contact with John by setting clear boundaries, not sleeping with him anymore, and getting rid of things that reminded me of him in my house were really important. I also found the 3 Ds especially helpful. When I look back at my first logs, I'm shocked by how flawed my thinking was. I made John out to be this perfect superhuman person in my own mind, which clearly wasn't accurate! In terms of early childhood learning, I'm still wrapping my head around it. I know that I internalized some traditional cultural beliefs about gender and romantic love that aren't serving me well. And I want to be more comfortable with intimacy moving forward, so I'm continuing to grapple with it. I haven't started dating again yet, but it's clear that I need to meet people who share my values and not pick them based on lust! I want to fall for someone who cares about family, loyalty, and community as much as I do, so I'm committed to making more value-based choices in my life, including in my romantic relationships.

Overall, my symptoms are improving pretty dramatically. I'm starting to enjoy my life again! I'm spending more time with friends, getting back into my favorite hobbies, taking care of my physical health, and generally less focused on John. I'm rebuilding my self-esteem by embracing the Truths from this book, remembering that I have value, I'm worthy of love, and just because John doesn't want me doesn't mean no one will. I loved John deeply and, in my heart of hearts, I want him to be happy. If that's not with me, it's better for both of us to move on. Maybe the most important thing that's changed about me is that I'm much stronger now than when I started this healing process. I know more about who I am, what I will and won't do in relationships moving forward, and what I want in a partner. That's truly a gift I'll take with me.

After writing your story of recovery, get your relationship story that you wrote in chapter 1 and compare the two. How does it feel to read your first story? How do your descriptions of yourself and your ex differ now? What's changed about you? What's stayed the same? Take some time to appreciate your growth and what you've learned from this experience.

As you look at your Exaholic Assessment Questionnaire results and your story of recovery, hopefully you see a meaningful improvement in most—if not all—of your symptoms. If you do, give yourself a round of applause, because your hard work is paying off. Moving forward, you don't want to lose any of the progress you've made! So, you'll want to be prepared to fight off symptoms that may pop up again in the future or that haven't improved as much as you'd like. Let's keep your healing momentum going while also preparing you to overcome setbacks.

Maintaining Your Growth and Tackling Setbacks

As you've undoubtedly experienced, moving on from an exaholic breakup requires a lot of effort. It takes tremendous determination and commitment to really evolve; change comes from becoming more aware of your symptoms, assessing what's driving them, and taking action to fight them on a daily basis! Your growth is the result of the compounding effect of the thousands of choices you make each day to help yourself heal. Change takes a lot of work! So, if you're worried that it's going to be this hard forever, let me reassure you that it gets easier over time. The goal of your recovery isn't for you to use these skills every single day for the rest of your life, just like the goal of therapy isn't to be in treatment forever! The goal is for you to understand your exaholic cycle and to know how to use CBT skills to stop your symptoms when they emerge so you feel in control of your experience, can sustain your well-being, and help yourself through tough times in the future.

The more you practice, the more second nature these skills become; at some point you'll use them habitually without thinking about it. After using the 3 Ds to challenge faulty thinking for a while, for example, you'll spot a red-flag thought when it pops into your mind and reframe it without even writing anything down. Similarly, as you get good at thought-stopping, you'll do it automatically when intrusive thinking patterns enter your mind. As you master these skills, they'll integrate into your way of being in the world and keep your exaholic symptoms at bay without much deliberate effort on your part. At some point—maybe today, tomorrow, or a year from now—you may not need to use any of these skills on a regular basis because your addiction to your ex won't be relevant to your life anymore!

That said, even if you're diligently practicing the skills in this book, you may have some lingering symptoms that aren't going away as quickly as you'd like. As with any addiction, it's very common to relapse or slip back into old patterns that jump-start the exaholic cycle (Melemis 2015; National

Institute on Drug Abuse 2019). Relapse can happen anytime but is especially common when you're confronted with an unexpected trigger related to your ex, like running into them or hearing that they're getting married. Relapse is also likely when you encounter a situation that leads to a dopamine hit or triggers feelings of being high, like starting to fall in love or being sexual with a new dating partner, even if the situation seemingly has nothing to do with your ex (Bobby 2015; Fisher 2016). So, it's important to think about future situations that may be tough for you—as you did when you explored your triggers in chapter 3—and plan for them so you don't spiral back into the exaholic cycle.

Some common situations that may make your symptoms flare up in the future include:

- Making unexpected contact with your ex

- Experiencing a major life transition (like a move, a new job, or the death of a loved one)

- Feeling especially stressed

- Dating or developing feelings for someone new

- Being sexually active with someone new

- Getting high from behaviors (like gambling) or substances (like alcohol or marijuana)

- Learning that your ex is getting married or in a serious relationship

- Hearing that your ex is really happy and living a more glamorous life now

If you find yourself triggered and notice a symptom reemerging, or if you're still struggling with a lingering symptom, your first step is to go back to using the CBT skills you learned in this book. Always start by filling out a self-monitoring log, because it's the quickest way to get detailed information about what's driving your symptoms: situations that trigger them, red-flag automatic thoughts that fuel them, and behavioral responses that make them worse. As you track your symptoms in your logs, practice the skills in this book as self-care interventions: cut off contact, use rumination time and thought-stopping, ride out your cravings, practice radical acceptance, consider the consequences of your behavior before you act, challenge faulty thinking and beliefs using the 3 Ds, put structure into your day, practice self-care, set healthy boundaries, and practice forgiveness. All of these CBT skills are designed to stop the cycle, so use them until your symptoms start to fade. And, if nothing seems to work, don't be afraid to experiment! The goal of CBT is to help you change your thought-feeling-behavior patterns in ways that improve your mental health (J. S. Beck 2021). So, try variations of any of these skills or experiment with new ones. If something you try doesn't help or makes you feel worse, use another self-care intervention until you find one that works.

The skills you learned in this book are really just a small introduction to the world of CBT interventions aimed at improving mental health symptoms (J. S. Beck 2021; Tolin 2016). If you found a particular topic really helpful or important during this healing journey, dive into it more deeply. For instance, you may want more information on developing healthy relationships, building self-esteem, understanding addiction, unpacking transgenerational patterns of learning, or exploring your multicultural makeup. Some topics that may help you explore your behavior in romantic relationships moving forward include:

- Codependency: exploring unhealthy psychological reliance on a romantic partner

- Early childhood learning and patterns of attachment: exploring how dynamics in your family of origin affected you and your adult relationships

- Healthy romantic relationships: learning to have meaningful and positive connections with lovers

- Self-esteem and self-efficacy: developing a stronger belief in your own worth and ability to influence your life

- Addiction: exploring how addictive tendencies—to your ex, other behaviors, or substances—affect you

- Spiritual or religious development: exploring your beliefs in a higher power

- Meditation and/or mindfulness: attending to your thoughts and feelings in the present moment without judgment

- Mental health struggles: working to heal other psychological symptoms, like depression, anxiety, or impulsive behaviors, that damage your well-being

- Radical honesty and self-deception: learning how to be honest with yourself and others

- Meaning: exploring how to create purpose in your life

I included some of my favorite resources at the back of this book, if you're interested. All are well worth your time, because letting go of your ex is part of a much larger lifelong journey of understanding yourself and making choices consistent with your values. As you move toward creating the next great chapter of your life, I'll leave you with a few final thoughts to keep you committed to your growth and well-being along the way.

Final Thoughts

Although this healing journey has been about letting go of your ex, at a deeper level it's been about understanding and transforming yourself. All of us need love to survive. It's biologically wired within us to be sexually attracted to others, form meaningful romantic connections, and bond with those we love the most. The more you can embrace every relationship as an opportunity to understand yourself more deeply, including this one, the more you can use that information to make choices that benefit you over time.

The truth is that letting go of your ex means coming to a place of internal peace from which you can honestly see them *without feeling any strong emotions*. Because the opposite of loving someone isn't hating them—it's being completely detached from and indifferent to them. You know you've really let go of your ex when you can look at the stark depictions of your breakup and have no reaction at all (Bobby 2015). For when you're honestly confronted with the most magically blissful, brutally painful, and passionately enraging moments you had with them and feel nothing, *you've taken your power back*. Then your ex no longer has any weight or pull on you anymore. Even better, eventually you may look back on this entire experience of love and loss with deep gratitude because it helped you grow into who you are today.

Taking an aerial view of your life map helps you let go of your ex because this vantage point makes this breakup feel less personal. As you disengage from the dramatic details of your breakup—the vivid images of heartache that you can still smell, taste, and touch as if they were happening to you right now—a more distant, panoramic viewpoint of your life map emerges. From way up high, you can see your entire road from birth until now. Your map is a continuation of your parents' and grandparents' maps, yet separate. As you grew, your map unfolded. Through your choices and life circumstances, your road intersected those of friends, peers, and eventually dating partners—all of whom operate independently because they're on their own life journeys.

Taking in your life from the highest viewpoint helps you see that everyone you encounter has their own stories of love and loss. Every human has a life map that you can't possibly understand or see in its entirety. And every single one of us has encountered twisty intersections with people who left us feeling pained when the relationship ended. Yet, in spite of our individual maps, we're also all interconnected. Every choice we make affects the lives of so many others. Often, we unknowingly pass our damaged baggage on to those we love the most. Your parents had their own pain, which they may have passed along to you in ways they didn't understand or couldn't see.

The struggles of your friends, peers, and dating partners may have manifested in ways that hurt you. And your ex is no exception; they have their own hurts and lessons to learn in this life. Although our internal battles are most obvious to us, everyone we encounter has their own battles, too. They affect us and we affect them as our roads intersect along the way.

So, as you move forward and continue to understand yourself in romantic relationships, strive to reflect the best of humanity. Develop empathy for everyone you meet because we're all on a learning journey in this life. We all make mistakes, and sometimes we hurt ourselves and others in the process. When you do, the goal is to learn from the experience, forgive errors, and do better moving forward. Harvest the wisdom of this breakup experience, because there were some gifts no matter how bad it seemed, and use this wisdom to move forward with grace and an open heart. Enter the world with compassion and treat others with respect even when they're impolite to you—not because they deserve to be respected, but because you're choosing to be your best self even if others aren't. Choose wisdom and growth over bitterness, even if you have a logically good reason to stay resentful. Don't let this breakup stop you from trying to find love again when you're ready. And always remember the fundamental Truth that you're valuable just as you are, with or without your ex.

Recommended Readings and Resources

Here are some resources you may find helpful on your healing journey:

- Developing healthy relationships: *Daring Greatly: How the Courage to Be Vulnerable Transforms the Way We Live, Love, Parent, and Lead*, by Brené Brown (2012); *Mating in Captivity: Unlocking Erotic Intelligence*, by Esther Perel (2017)

- Codependency: *Codependent No More: How to Stop Controlling Others and Start Caring for Yourself*, 2nd ed., by Melody Beattie (2022); *Facing Codependence: What It Is, Where It Comes From, and How It Sabotages Our Lives*, by Pia Mellody, Andrea Wells Miller, and J. Keith Miller (2003)

- Love addiction: *Anatomy of Love: A Natural History of Mating, Marriage, and Why We Stray*, by Helen Fisher (2016); *Exaholics: Breaking Your Addiction to an Ex Love*, by Lisa Marie Bobby (2015); or a group like CoDA (https://coda.org)

- Spiritual or religious exploration: *There's a Spiritual Solution to Every Problem*, by Wayne Dyer (2003); *Sacred Contracts: Awakening Your Divine Potential*, by Caroline Myss (2003)

- Early childhood learning and patterns of attachment: *Attached: The New Science of Adult Attachment and How It Can Help You Find—and Keep—Love*, by Amir Levine and Rachel Heller (2012)

- Building self-esteem and self-efficacy: *Ten Days to Self-Esteem*, by David Burns (1993); *The Feeling Good Handbook*, by David Burns (1999)

- Overcoming other mental health struggles (like anxiety and depression): *The CBT Toolbox*, 2nd ed., by Jeff Riggenback (2021); *The Negative Thoughts Workbook: CBT Skills to Overcome the Repetitive Worry, Shame, and Rumination That Drive Anxiety and Depression*, by David Clark (2020)

- Developing life meaning and purpose: *Man's Search for Meaning: An Introduction to Logotherapy*, by Viktor Frankl (1962)

- Practicing forgiveness: *Forgiveness Is a Choice: A Step-by-Step Process for Resolving Anger and Restoring Hope*, by Robert Enright (2001)

References

Ainsworth, M. S. 1989. "Attachments Beyond Infancy." *American Psychologist* 44: 709–16.

Alcoholics Anonymous World Services, Inc. 2003. *Twelve Steps and Twelve Traditions.* New York: Alcoholics Anonymous World Services, Inc.

American Psychological Association. 2002. *Developing Adolescents: A Reference for Professionals.* Washington, DC: American Psychological Association. https://www.apa.org/pi/families/resources/develop.pdf.

Anda, R. F., V. J. Felitti, J. D. Bremner, J. D. Walker, C. Whitfield, B. D. Perry, S. R. Dube, and W. H. Giles. 2006. "The Enduring Effects of Abuse and Related Adverse Experiences in Childhood: A Convergence of Evidence from Neurobiology and Epidemiology." *European Archives of Psychiatry and Clinical Neuroscience* 256: 174–86.

Asensio, S., V. Hernández-Rabaza, and J. V. Orón Semper. 2020. "What Is the 'Trigger' of Addiction?" *Frontiers of Behavioral Neuroscience* 14. https://doi.org/10.3389/fnbeh.2020.00054.

Ashe, M. L., M. G. Newman, and S. J. Wilson. 2015. "Delay Discounting and the Use of Mindful Attention Versus Distraction in the Treatment of Drug Addiction: A Conceptual Review." *Journal of Experimental Analysis of Behavior* 103: 234–48.

Bakhshani, N. M. 2014. "Impulsivity: A Predisposition Toward Risky Behaviors." *International Journal of High Risk Behaviors and Addiction* 3: e20428. https://doi.org/10.5812/ijhrba.20428.

Bandura, A. 1977. *Social Learning Theory.* Englewood Cliffs, NJ: Prentice-Hall.

Barutcu, K. F., and Y. C. Aydin. 2013. "The Scale for Emotional Reactions Following the Breakup." *Procedia—Social and Behavioral Sciences* 84: 786–90.

Baumeister, R. F., S. R. Wotman, and A. M. Stillwell. 1993. "Unrequited Love: On Heartbreak, Anger, Guilt, Scriptlessness, and Humiliation." *Journal of Personality and Social Psychology* 64: 377–94.

Beck, A. T. 1976. *Cognitive Therapy and the Emotional Disorders.* New York: International Universities Press.

Beck, A. T., A. J. Rush, B. F. Shaw, and G. Emery. 1979. *Cognitive Therapy of Depression.* New York: Guilford Press.

Beck, J. S. 2021. *Cognitive Behavior Therapy: Basics and Beyond.* 3rd ed. New York: Guilford Press.

Blum, K., A. L. C. Chen, J. Giordano, J. Borsten, T. J. H. Chen, M. Hauser, T. Simpatico, J. Femino, E. R. Braverman, and D. Barh. 2012. "The Addictive Brain: All Roads Lead to Dopamine." *Journal of Psychoactive Drugs* 44: 134–43.

Bobby, L. M. 2015. *Exaholics: Breaking Your Addiction to an Ex Love.* New York: Sterling.

Bowlby, J. 1971. *Attachment: Attachment and Loss.* New York: Penguin Books.

Bretherton, I. 1992. "The Origins of Attachment Theory: John Bowlby and Mary Ainsworth." *Developmental Psychology* 28: 759–75.

Chrystal, M., J. A. Karl, and R. Fischer. 2019. "The Complexities of 'Minding the Gap': Perceived Discrepancies Between Values and Behavior Affect Well-Being." *Frontiers in Psychology* 10. https://doi.org/10.3389/fpsyg.2019.00736.

Clark, D. A. 2020. *The Negative Thoughts Workbook: CBT Skills to Overcome the Repetitive Worry, Shame, and Rumination That Drive Anxiety and Depression.* Oakland, CA: New Harbinger.

Cloud, H., and J. S. Townsend. 2000. *Boundaries in Dating: How Healthy Choices Grow Healthy Relationships.* Grand Rapids, MI: Zondervan.

Cloud, H., and J. S. Townsend. 2017. *Boundaries: When to Say Yes, How to Say No to Take Control of Your Life.* Grand Rapids, MI: Zondervan.

Costa, S., N. Barberis, M. D. Griffiths, L. Benedetto, and M. Ingrassia. 2019. "The Love Addiction Inventory: Preliminary Findings of the Development Process and Psychometric Characteristics." *International Journal of Mental Health and Addiction* 19: 651–68.

Davis, M., E. R. Eshelman, and M. McKay. 1988. *The Relaxation and Stress Reduction Workbook.* 3rd ed. Oakland, CA: New Harbinger.

Earp, B. D., O. A. Wudarczyk, B. Foddy, and J. Savulescu. 2017. "Addicted to Love: What Is Love Addiction and When Should It Be Treated?" *Philosophy, Psychiatry, and Psychology* 24: 77–92.

Ellis, A., and R. A. Harper. 1997. *A Guide to Rational Living.* 3rd ed. Woodland Hills, CA: Melvin Powers Wilshire Book Company.

Enright, R. D. 2001. *Forgiveness Is a Choice: A Step-by-Step Process for Resolving Anger and Restoring Hope.* Washington, DC: American Psychological Association.

Field, T. 2017. "Romantic Breakup Distress, Betrayal and Heartbreak: A Review." *International Journal of Behavioral Research and Psychology* 5: 217–25.

Field, T., M. Diego, M. Pelaez, O. Deeds, and J. Delgado. 2011. "Breakup Distress in University Students: A Review." *College Student Journal* 45: 461–80.

Filbey, F. M. 2019. *The Neuroscience of Addiction.* UK: Cambridge University Press.

Fisher, H. E. 2004. *Why We Love: The Nature and Chemistry of Romantic Love.* New York: Henry Holt.

Fisher, H. E. 2016. *Anatomy of Love: A Natural History of Mating, Marriage, and Why We Stray.* Rev. and upd. ed. New York: W. W. Norton.

Fisher, H. E., A. Aron, and L. L. Brown. 2005. "Romantic Love: An fMRI Study of a Neural Mechanism for Mate Choice." *Journal of Comparative Neurology* 493: 58–62.

Fisher, H. E., A. Aron, D. Mashek, H. Li, and L. L. Brown. 2002. "Defining the Brain Systems of Lust, Romantic Attraction, and Attachment." *Archives of Sexual Behavior* 31: 413–19.

Fisher, H. E., X. Xu, A. Aron, and L. L. Brown. 2016. "Intense, Passionate, Romantic Love: A Natural Addiction? How the Fields that Investigate Romance and

Substance Abuse Can Inform Each Other." *Frontiers in Psychology* 7. http://doi.org/10.3389/fpsyg.2016.00687.

Fox, J., and R. S. Tokunaga. 2015. "Romantic Partner Monitoring After Breakups: Attachment, Dependence, Distress, and Post-Dissolution Online Surveillance via Social Networking Sites." *Cyberpsychology, Behavior, and Social Networking* 18: 491–98.

Francoeur, A., T. Lecomte, I. Daigneault, A. Brassard, V. Lecours, and C. Hache-Labelle. 2020. "Social Cognition as Mediator of Romantic Breakup Adjustment in Young Adults Who Experienced Childhood Maltreatment." *Journal of Aggression, Maltreatment, and Trauma* 29: 1125–42.

Frankl, V. 1962. *Man's Search for Meaning: An Introduction to Logotherapy.* Rev. and enl. ed. Boston: Beacon Press.

Freud, A. 1937. *The Ego and the Mechanisms of Defense.* London: Hogarth Press.

Freud, S. (1894) 2013. *The Neuro-Psychoses of Defence.* N.p.: Read Books, Ltd.

Grant J. E., M. N. Potenza, A. Weinstein, and D. A. Gorelick. 2010. "Introduction to Behavioral Addictions." *American Journal of Drug and Alcohol Abuse* 36: 233–41.

Halpern-Meekin S., W. D. Manning, P. C. Giordano, and M. A. Longmore. 2013. "Relationship Churning in Emerging Adulthood: On/Off Relationships and Sex with an Ex." *Journal of Adolescent Research* 28: 166–88.

Harandi, T. F., M. M. Taghinasab, and T. D. Nayeri. 2017. "The Correlation of Social Support with Mental Health: A Meta-Analysis." *Electron Physician* 9: 5212–22.

Harlow, H. F. 1958. "The Nature of Love." *American Psychologist* 13: 673–85.

Hayes. S. C., K. D. Strosahl, and K. G. Wilson. 2012. *Acceptance and Commitment Therapy: The Process and Practice of Mindful Change.* 2nd ed. New York: Guilford Press.

Hazan, C., and P. R. Shafer. 1987. "Romantic Love Conceptualized as an Attachment Process." *Journal of Personality and Social Psychology* 52: 511–41.

Heshmati, R., M. Zemestani, and A. Vujanovic. 2021. "Associations of Childhood Maltreament and Attachment Styles with Romantic Breakup Grief Severity: The Role of Emotional Suppression." *Journal of Interpersonal Violence* 37. https://doi.org/10.1177%2F0886260521997438.

Hofmann, S. G., A. Asnaani, I. J. J. Vonk, A. T. Sawyer, and A. Fang. 2012. "The Efficacy of Cognitive Behavioral Therapy: A Review of Meta-Analyses." *Cognitive Therapy and Research* 36: 427–40.

Hughes, K., M. A. Bellis, K. A. Hardcastle, D. Sethi, A. Butchart, C. Mikton, L. Jones, and M. P. Dunne. 2017. "The Effect of Multiple Adverse Childhood Experiences on Health: A Systematic Review and Meta-Analysis." *Lancet Public Health* 2: e356–366. http://doi.org/10.1016/S2468-2667(17)30118-4.

Jonason, P. K., J. R. Garcia, G. D. Webster, N. P. Li, and H. E. Fisher. 2015. "Relationship Dealbreakers: Traits People Avoid in Potential Mates." *Personality and Social Psychology Bulletin* 41. https://doi.org/10.1177/0146167215609064.

Kail, R. V., and J. C. Cavanaugh. 2010. *Human Development: A Life-Span View.* 5th ed. Belmont, CA: Wadsworth Cengage Learning.

Kansky, J., and J. P. Allen. 2018. "Making Sense and Moving On: The Potential for Individual and Interpersonal Growth Following Emerging Adult Breakups." *Emerging Adulthood* 6: 172–90.

Kesberg, R., and J. Keller. 2018. "The Relation Between Human Values and Perceived Situation Characteristics in Everyday Life." *Frontiers in Psychology* 9. http://doi.org/10.3389/fpsyg.2018.01676.

Kim, H. S., D. C. Hodgins, B. Kim, and T. C. Wild. 2020. "Transdiagnostic or Disorder Specific? Indicators of Substance and Behavioral Addictions Nominated by People with Lived Experience." *Journal of Clinical Medicine* 9. https://doi.org/10.3390/jcm9020334.

Kirouac, M., and K. Witkiewitz. 2017. "Identifying 'Hitting Bottom' Among Individuals with Alcohol Problems: Development and Evaluation of the Noteworthy Aspects of Drinking Important to Recovery (NADIR)." *Substance Use and Misuse* 52: 1602–15.

Koob, G. F., and N. D. Volkow. 2010. "Neurocircuitry of Addiction." *Neuropsychopharmacology* 35: 217–38.

Kwako, L. E., and G. F. Koob. 2017. "Neuroclinical Framework for the Role of Stress in Addiction." *Chronic Stress* 1. https://doi.org/10.1177/2470547017698140.

Kübler-Ross, E. 2014. *On Death and Dying: What the Dying Have to Teach Doctors, Nurses, Clergy, and Their Own Families.* 50th anniv. ed. New York: Scribner.

Lepore, S. J., and M. A. Greenberg. 2002. "Mending Broken Hearts: Effects of Expressive Writing on Mood, Cognitive Processing, Social Adjustment, and Health Following a Relationship Breakup." *Psychology and Health* 17: 547–60.

Levine, A., and R. S. F. Heller. 2012. *Attached: The New Science of Adult Attachment and How It Can Help You Find—and Keep—Love.* New York: TarcherPerigee.

Linehan, M. M. 2014. *DBT Skills Training Manual.* 2nd ed. New York: Guilford Press.

Luigjes, J., V. Lorenzetti, S. de Haan, G. J. Youssef, C. Murawski, Z. Sjoerds, W. van den Brink, D. Denys, L. F. Fontenelle, and M. Yücel. 2019. "Defining Compulsive Behavior." *Neuropsychological Review* 29: 4–13.

Marshall, T. C. 2012. "Facebook Surveillance of Former Romantic Partners: Associations with Postbreakup Recovery and Personal Growth." *Cyberpsychology, Behavior, and Social Networking* 15: 521–26.

Marwood, L., T. Wise, A. M. Perkins, and A. J. Cleare. 2018. "Meta-Analyses of the Neural Mechanisms and Predictors of Response to Psychotherapy in Depression and Anxiety." *Neuroscience and Biobehavioral Reviews* 95: 61–72.

Melemis, S. M. 2015. "Relapse Prevention and the Five Rules of Recovery." *Yale Journal of Biological Medicine* 88: 325–32.

Mellody, P., A. W. Miller, and J. K. Miller. 2003. *Facing Love Addiction: Giving Yourself the Power to Change the Way You Love.* New York: HarperOne.

Miller, W. R., ed. 1999. *Integrating Spirituality into Treatment: Resources for Practitioners.* Washington, DC: American Psychological Association.

Myss, C. 2008. *Entering the Castle: Finding the Inner Path to God and Your Soul's Purpose.* New York: Free Press.

National Institute on Drug Abuse. 2019. *Genetics and Epigenetics of Addiction DrugFacts.* https://nida.nih.gov/publications/drugfacts/genetics-epigenetics-addiction.

National Institute on Drug Abuse. 2020. *Drugs, Brains, and Behavior: The Science of Addiction.* https://nida.nih.gov/sites/default/files/soa.pdf.

Norcross, J. C., P. M. Krebs, and J. O. Prochaska. 2011. "Stages of Change." *Journal of Clinical Psychology* 67: 143–54.

O'Sullivan, L. F., K. Hugest, F. Talbot, and R. Fuller. 2019. "Plenty of Fish in the Ocean: How do Traits Reflecting Resiliency Moderate Adjustment After Experiencing a Romantic Breakup in Emerging Adulthood?" *Journal of Youth and Adolescence* 48: 949–62.

Oyserman, D. 2015. "Psychology of Values." In *International Encyclopedia of the Social and Behavioral Sciences,* 2nd ed., vol. 25, edited by J. D. Wright. Oxford: Elsevier.

Peele, S., and A. Brodsky. 1975. *Love and Addiction.* New York: Taplinger.

Perilloux, C., and D. M. Buss. 2008. "Breaking Up Romantic Relationships: Costs Experienced and Coping Strategies Deployed." *Evolutionary Psychology* 6: 164–81.

Ponizovskiy, V., L. Grigoryan, U. Kühnen, and K. Boehnke. 2019. "Social Construction of the Value-Behavior Relation." *Frontiers in Psychology* 10. https://doi.org/10.3389/fpsyg.2019.00934.

Primeau, J. E., H. L. Servaty-Seib, and D. Enersen. 2013. "Type of Writing Task and College Students' Meaning Making Following a Romantic Breakup." *Journal of College Counseling* 16: 32–48.

Regan, P. C., S. Lakhanpal, and C. Anguiano. 2012. "Relationship Outcomes in Indian-American Love-Based and Arranged Marriages." *Psychological Reports* 110: 915–24.

Reimer, J. E., and A. R. Estrada. 2021. "College Students' Grief over a Breakup." *Journal of Loss and Trauma* 26: 179–91.

Reynaud, M., L. Karila, L. Blecha, and A. Benyamina. 2010. "Is Love Passion an Addictive Disorder?" *American Journal of Drug and Alcohol Abuse* 35: 261–67.

Roberts, K. A. 2002. "Stalking Following the Breakup of Romantic Relationships: Characteristics of Stalking Former Partners." *Journal of Forensic Sciences* 47: 1070–77.

Rokeach, M. 1973. *The Nature of Human Values.* New York: Free Press.

Sanches, M., and V. P. John. 2019. "Treatment of Love Addiction: Current Status and Perspectives." *European Journal of Psychiatry* 33: 38–44.

Schwartz, S. H. 1992. "Universals in the Content and Structure of Values: Theoretical Advances and Empirical Tests in 20 Countries." In *Advances in Experimental Social Psychology,* vol. 25, edited by M. P. Zanna. London: Academic Press.

Skinner, B. F. 1974. *About Behaviorism.* New York: Knopf.

Starcke, K., S. Antons, P. Trotzke, and M. Brand. 2018. "Cue-Reactivity in Behavioral Addiction: A Meta-Analysis and Methodological Considerations." *Journal of Behavioral Addictions* 7: 227–38.

Sue, D. W., and D. Sue. 2012. *Counseling the Culturally Diverse: Theory and Practice.* 6th ed. Hoboken, NJ: John Wiley and Sons.

Sussman, S. 2010. "Love Addiction: Definition, Etiology, Treatment." *Sexual Addiction and Compulsivity* 17: 31–45.

Sussman, S., N. Lisha, and M. Griffiths. 2011. "Prevalence of the Addictions: A Problem of the Majority or the Minority?" *Evaluation and the Health Professions* 34: 3–56.

Tobore, T. O. 2020. "Towards a Comprehensive Theory of Love: The Quadruple Theory." *Frontiers in Psychology* 11. https://doi.org/10.3389/fpsyg.2020.00862.

Tolin, D. F. 2016. *Doing CBT: A Comprehensive Guide to Working with Behaviors, Thoughts, and Emotions.* New York: Guilford Press.

Uckelstam, C.-J., B. Philips, R. Holmqvist, and F. Falkenström. 2019. "Prediction of Treatment Outcome in Psychotherapy by Client Initial Symptom Distress Profiles." *Journal of Counseling Psychology* 66: 736–46.

Van der Watt, A. S. J., A. Roos, S. du Plessis, E. Bui, E. Lesch, and S. Seedat. 2021. "An Attachment Theory Approach to Reframing Romantic Relationship Breakups in University Students: A Narrative Review of Attachment, Neural Circuitry, and Posttraumatic Stress Symptoms." *Journal of Couple and Relationship Therapy* 21. https://doi.org/10.1080/15332691.2021.1908197.

Von Hammerstein, C., A. Cornil, S. Rothen, L. Romo, Y. Khazaal, A. Benyamina, J. Billieux, and A. Luquiens. 2020. "Psychometric Properties of the Transaddiction Craving Triggers Questionnaire in Alcohol Use Disorder." *International Journal of Methods in Psychiatric Research* 29: e1815. https://doi.org/10.1002/mpr.1815.

Warren, C. S., and L. M. Akoury. 2020. "Emphasizing the 'Cultural' in Sociocultural: A Systematic Review of Research on Thin-Ideal Internalization, Acculturation, and Eating Pathology in US Ethnic Minorities." *Psychology Research and Behavior Management* 13: 319–30.

Yalom, I. D. 1980. *Existential Psychotherapy.* New York: Basic Books.

Young, E. S., J. S. Klosko, and M. E. Weishaar. 2003. *Schema Therapy: A Practitioner's Guide.* New York: Guilford Press.

Young, E. S., J. A., Simpson, V. Griskevicius, C. O. Huelsnitz, and C. Fleck. 2019. "Childhood Attachment and Adult Personality: A Life History Perspective." *Self and Identity* 18: 22–38.

Zarate, D., M. Ball, C. Montag, M. Prokofieva, and V. Stavropoulos. 2022. "Unravelling the Web of Addictions: A Network Analysis Approach." *Addictive Behaviors Reports* 15:100406. https://doi.org/10.1016/j.abrep.2022.100406 .

Cortney Soderlind Warren, PhD, ABPP, is a board-certified clinical psychologist; and former tenured associate professor of psychology at the University of Nevada, Las Vegas (UNLV). Having won numerous professional awards for her research, Warren is an expert on addictions, eating pathology, self-deception, and the practice of psychotherapy from a cross-cultural perspective. In addition to her academic work, Warren is a speaker, author, and coach with a passion for bringing psychological tools to the public. She earned her doctorate from Texas A&M University after completing a clinical internship at McLean Hospital/Harvard Medical School in 2006.

Foreword writer **Antonio Cepeda-Benito, PhD,** has published extensively, received several awards, and his research connecting the disciplines of behavioral neuroscience and clinical psychology to investigate drug addiction and eating disorders from a cross-cultural perspective has been supported by grants from the National Institute on Drug Abuse, the Texas Department of Health, and the Spanish Ministry of Science and Technology. In 2009, he was named one of the "Top 100 Most Influential Hispanics" by *Hispanic Business Magazine*.

Real change *is* possible

For more than forty-five years, New Harbinger has published proven-effective self-help books and pioneering workbooks to help readers of all ages and backgrounds improve mental health and well-being, and achieve lasting personal growth. In addition, our spirituality books offer profound guidance for deepening awareness and cultivating healing, self-discovery, and fulfillment.

Founded by psychologist Matthew McKay and Patrick Fanning, New Harbinger is proud to be an independent, employee-owned company. Our books reflect our core values of integrity, innovation, commitment, sustainability, compassion, and trust. Written by leaders in the field and recommended by therapists worldwide, New Harbinger books are practical, accessible, and provide real tools for real change.

 **newharbinger**publications

MORE BOOKS from
NEW HARBINGER PUBLICATIONS

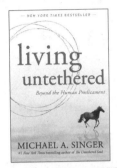

THE EMOTIONALLY EXHAUSTED WOMAN

Why You're Feeling Depleted and How to Get What You Need

978-1648480157 / US $18.95

LIVING UNTETHERED

Beyond the Human Predicament

978-1648480935 / US $18.95

ADULT CHILDREN OF EMOTIONALLY IMMATURE PARENTS

How to Heal from Distant, Rejecting, or Self-Involved Parents

978-1626251700 / US $18.95

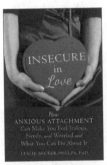

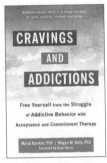

INSECURE IN LOVE

How Anxious Attachment Can Make You Feel Jealous, Needy, and Worried and What You Can Do About It

978-1608828159 / US $17.95

CRAVINGS AND ADDICTIONS

Free Yourself from the Struggle of Addictive Behavior with Acceptance and Commitment Therapy

978-1684038336 / US $17.95

STOP OVERTHINKING YOUR RELATIONSHIP

Break the Cycle of Anxious Rumination to Nurture Love, Trust, and Connection with Your Partner

978-1648480034 / US $18.95

🌱 **new**harbinger**publications**

1-800-748-6273 / newharbinger.com

(VISA, MC, AMEX / prices subject to change without notice)

Follow Us 📷 📘 🐦 ▶ 📌 🔗

Don't miss out on new books from New Harbinger.
Subscribe to our email list at **newharbinger.com/subscribe** 🖱

Did you know there are **free tools** you can download for this book?

Free tools are things like **worksheets, guided meditation exercises**, and **more** that will help you get the most out of your book.

You can download free tools for this book—whether you bought or borrowed it, in any format, from any source—from the New Harbinger website. All you need is a NewHarbinger.com account. Just use the URL provided in this book to view the free tools that are available for it. Then, click on the "download" button for the free tool you want, and follow the prompts that appear to log in to your NewHarbinger.com account and download the material.

You can also save the free tools for this book to your **Free Tools Library** so you can access them again anytime, just by logging in to your account! Just look for this button on the book's free tools page.

+ Save this to my free tools library

If you need help accessing or downloading free tools, visit **newharbinger.com/faq** or contact us at **customerservice@newharbinger.com**.